SCORE, FOLD, CREATE!

By Diana Crick, Penny Wessenauer and Friends

Contents

Scor-Pal® Version 3

The slightly textured scoring surface is 12 x 12 inches and light blue in color. There are grooves at every ⅛ inch, plus ⅛-inch grooves for the first and last inch of the board and specialty grooves. A free Scor-Tool is included in the snap-in holder. **Note**: *If you have Version 2, gray in color, you will still be able to make the projects. However, you will have to move the left-hand edge of the paper away from the left fence to achieve ⅛-inch scores.*

Scor-Buddy™

The Scor-Buddy was designed for card makers on the go and has grooves every ¼ inch across the board, plus ⅛-inch grooves for the first and last inch of the board and specialty grooves. It measures approximately 9 x 7½ inches and has a fence down the left side. A free Scor-Tool is included in the snap-in holder, and it comes with its own faux ultra-suede carry tote.

A lot of the projects can be made with the Scor-Buddy. You will need the Scor-Pal for longer scores.

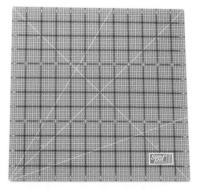

Scor-Mat™

The translucent Scor-Mat fits exactly in the recessed area of your Scor-Pal. It is almost 12 x 12 inches. On one side is a self-healing cutting mat with ⅛-inch increments in white and 1-inch markings in black. The mat is invaluable when you have to accurately mark measurements on cardstock. We recommend the use of a sharp craft knife rather than a rotary cutter. The other side is a shiny work surface. Zip Dry™ Glue and Scor-Tape can easily be removed from this surface. The mat does not have a silicon backing. Do not apply direct heat from any source, such as a hot embossing gun or hot-glue gun. After scoring, there's no need to put your Scor-Pal away, simply insert the Scor-Mat and continue crafting.

Scor-Bug™

The Scor-Bug is a rotary tool that embosses a row of pearl-like little bumps, adding texture and relief to your cardstock. The reverse side becomes a straight row of little depressions that look like piercings. Simply run the engaged rotary Scor-Bug up the groove of your Scor-Pal over the cardstock.

Stay Put Craft Mat™

As it states, it stays put on practically any work surface; no more sliding around, having to use glue dots or holding it in place with your hand. The unique backing forms an airtight seal without harm to your work surface, leaving your hands free for crafting.

The mat has a nonstick surface and is heat resistant. It can be used with, to name just a few, hot glue, molten UTEE, alcohol inks, paints, etc. To clean, simply wash the mat in hot, soapy water. The special backing does not wear off. The mat measures 15¾ x 19¾ inches.

It is a must-have when you are making rosettes.

Scor-Tape™

Scor-Tape is a premium, double-sided adhesive that is acid-free, heat resistant and incredibly sticky. Its tight bond makes it the perfect permanent adhesive for making cards, boxes and books, and it works ideally for the iris-folding technique. Scor-Tape can also be used with embossing powders, foils, beads, glitter, ribbon and other embellishments. Unlike other tapes, Scor-Tape is paper backed, which means you can tear it with your thumb and finger—no need for scissors or sharp blades. The paper backing is also eco-friendly. All rolls are 27 yards long, so they are an exceptional value. The tapes come in ⅛-inch, ¼-inch, ½-inch, 1-inch, 1½-inch, 2-inch and 2½-inch-width sizes. There are also 6 x 6-inch sheets and 8½ x 11-inch sheets that are perfect for making die cuts to glitter or emboss.

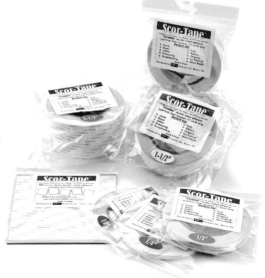

Scor-Pal® Basics

[Photo 1]

[Photo 2]

[Photo 3]

The Scor-Tool is specially shaped below the tip on either edge to fit the contour of the scoring grooves on the Scor-Pal. For best results, hold the tool at a 45-degree angle to the surface, *not* on the tip, as you would hold a pencil (Photo 1). **Note:** *When scoring thinner papers, make sure to apply light pressure as pressing too hard can cut paper instead of scoring it.*

Use even pressure and draw the tool down the paper. If you are using a heavy-weight cardstock or are embossing for decorative purposes, you may want to go twice over the score (Photo 2).

If you are scoring patterned paper or cardstock with a white core, lower the angle of the Scor-Tool even more to avoid cracking or cutting through your paper.

To clean the Scor-Pal, use warm soapy water, then rinse and dry thoroughly.

Features of the Scor-Pal

In the tutorials the instructions will state, for example, "With long edge at top fence"—this always means to align paper to **left fence** and **top fence** (Photo 3).

The top fence includes a 12-inch ruler with standard ruler markings and grooves every ¼ inch across the width and ⅛-inch grooves at the first and last inch.

Left fence includes standard ruler with measurements at every ½ inch.

Special symbols are also included in the top fence to indicate scoring points to quickly create a common A2 card, a gatefold or tri-fold card.

An Asterisk * is located on the 4¼-inch groove, which would be the center point on an 8½-inch base used for a common A2 card.

Dots are included at the 2⅛- and 6⅜-inch marks and are used to create a gatefold card from an 8½-inch-wide card base.

Two Inverted Triangles indicate the scoring points to make quick and easy work of creating professional-looking brochures or tri-fold cards from an 11-inch-wide paper (only one asterisk is included on Scor-Buddy).

Double Arrows at the bottom of the 6-inch groove indicate the correct alignment when making diagonal scores.

Diana Crick's signature at the top of the board covers a magnetized area to hold brads, paper clips, etc.

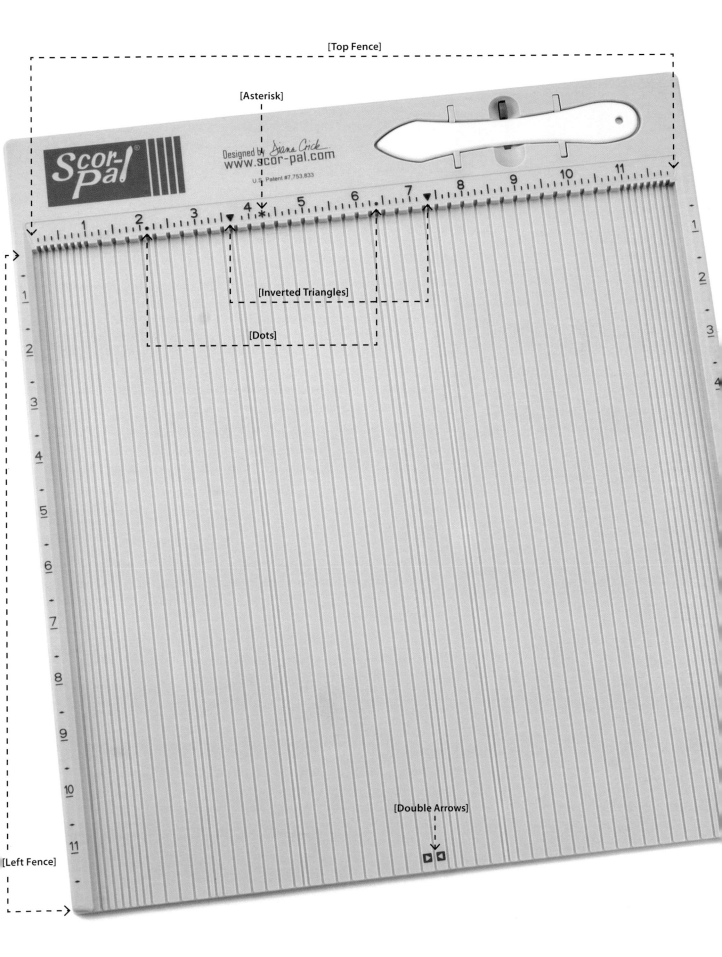

[Top Fence]

[Asterisk]

Designed by *Diana Crick*
www.scor-pal.com

U.S. Patent #7,753,833

Scor-Pal®

[Inverted Triangles]

[Dots]

[Double Arrows]

[Left Fence]

[Photo 5]

Paper Grain

When possible, always score with the "grain" of the paper. Cup the paper in your hands, bringing the sides together. If the paper bends easily the grain is lengthways. Turn the paper in the other direction and repeat same action. You will feel a slight resistance. On an 8½-inch sheet of cardstock the grain usually runs down the 11-inch length.

When working with a 12 x 12-inch sheet of cardstock, always test for the paper grain.

Direction of Fold & Accordion Folds

Always fold your card so the debossed score line is on the outside of the fold and the embossed ridge is on the inside of the fold (Photo 5).

When you score the paper you are spreading the paper fibers for the fold. If you fold in the other direction, you are squashing the paper fibers you just bent. For accordion folds you must alternate the side of the paper you score on. For example, to create an accordion fold with 1-inch folds, score at odd numbers—1 inch, 3 inches, 5 inches, 7 inches, 9 inches and 11 inches on the right side of the paper. Turn the paper over, top to bottom, and score at even numbers—2 inches, 4 inches, 6 inches, 8 inches and 10 inches (Photo 6).

[Photo 6]

The embossed score lines on the right side of the paper will fold downward to form what is commonly referred to as valley folds. The debossed folds on the right side will extend upward to form mountain folds.

Tip: When making multiple A2 cards, score the full 11 inches at 4¼ inches, then cut cardstock at 5½ inches. This way you are saving time by scoring only once to make two cards.

Scoring at ⅛-Inch Intervals

When Version 3 of the Scor-Pal—blue with grooves at every ¼-inch mark plus specialty grooves—was being designed, it was decided not to have grooves at every ⅛-inch interval to give the scoring surface better clarity making it easier to read.

When making ⅛-inch scores such as at 3⅝ inches, you will move the left side of the paper away from the left fence.

For a ⅝-inch score, count back five grooves and position the left edge of the paper at the middle of that groove.

Always go up one full number—so score at 4 inches (Photo 7).

[Photo 7]

It is always two steps: Step one, count backward for eighths; and Step 2, go up one full number for your score line. You go up one number because you are losing the first inch by using it for the eighth measurement. For example, for 7⅜ inches, count back 3 and score at 8-inch mark; for 5⅞ inches, count back 7 and score at 6-inch mark.

Scoring Techniques & Terminology

By **Julie Koerber**

Scoring Techniques
Embossing and debossing adds wonderful texture to your backgrounds, or can be the focal point of your card.

Materials
› Scor-Pal or Scor-Buddy
› Scor-Bug
› Distress inks or other inks
› Metallic rub-on paint
› Sanding block
› Craft sponge

Crisscross
Place paper square on the diagonal, aligning top point and bottom point on the 6-inch groove. Score at 5½-inch, 5¾-inch, 6-inch, 6¼-inch and 6½-inch marks. Flip your paper 90 degrees so that the opposite corners sit on the 6-inch mark. Again, score at 5½-inch, 5¾-inch, 6-inch, 6¼-inch and 6½-inch marks. **Note:** *The example paper was turned over and the embossed lines were gently sanded to reveal the paper's white core.*

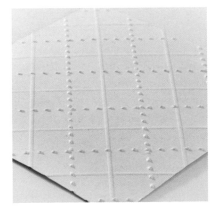

Argyle
Place paper square right side down, aligning top point and bottom point on the 6-inch mark. Score at the 4-inch, 5-inch, 6-inch, 7-inch and 8-inch marks. Move your paper away from the top fence so you are using the middle of the board, still aligned on the 6-inch mark. Using the Scor-Bug, roll the tool up or down following the grooves at 4½-inch, 5½-inch, 6½-inch and 7½-inch marks. Turn your paper 90 degrees, line your upper right and lower left corners along the 6-inch mark and repeat scoring instructions.

Chair Rail Border

Align top-left corner of cardstock in top-left corner of the Scor-Pal. Score across the width of the paper at the center; move scoring tool ¼ inch to the right and score paper again. Turn the paper 90 degrees clockwise and score at every ½-inch mark, bringing your Scor-Tool from the top of the paper down to the first horizontal score line. *Note: This could be the bottom of the card if using to create a card front.* Rescore the horizontal lines to improve the overall look.

Pillow Ticking

Align top-left corner of cardstock in top-left corner of the Scor-Pal. Score on the wrong side of the paper at every ½-inch mark across the width of paper. Using the Scor-Bug tool, start at the ¼-inch mark on the board and score every ½ inch. Perforated score lines will be at ¼-inch, ¾-inch, 1¼-inch mark, etc., covering the entire width of the paper.

Box Plaid

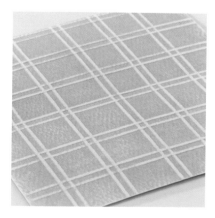

Align edge of the paper on the 1½-inch mark and score at 2 inches and 2⅛ inches (dot). Move your paper so that the last line you scored sits on the 1½-inch mark and repeat. Keep moving the paper so that the last scored line sits on the 1½-inch mark to repeat the pattern. Turn paper 90 degrees clockwise and repeat scoring instructions. Embossed lines on the sample were sanded to reveal the paper's white core.

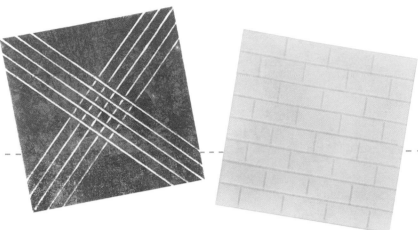

Plaid

Align top-left corner of cardstock in top-left corner of the Scor-Pal; score every 1 inch across the width of your paper. Using the Scor-Bug tool, score at the ½-inch mark and continue scoring every 1 inch so that the Scor-Bug perforated marks travel in between the scored lines. Repeat across the entire width of the paper. Turn the paper 90 degrees clockwise and repeat scoring instructions.

Sunbeams

Line opposite corners of your paper on the 6-inch mark and score. To create your sunbeams, you will move only the bottom corner by ½ inch and score again. The top corner will stay on the 6-inch mark. Repeat this by moving the bottom corner ½ inch each time. Repeat in the opposite direction in order to get the full sunbeam effect.

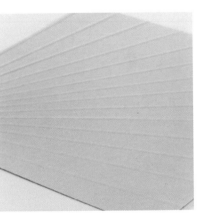

Spotlight

Using a shaped die as your guide, center your die and emboss using your machine of choice. Place paper facedown on your Scor-Pal and score vertically every ¼ inch, making sure your Scor-Tool stops and starts on either side of your embossed shape. Use the clean and un-embossed area as a canvas for a sentiment or stamped image. ***Note:*** *In the example, the paper was turned over when finished and the embossed lines were lightly sanded to create a more distressed look. You would need a paper with a white core to achieve this look.*

Brick Road

Score your paper every ½ inch with the right side of your paper facedown. Turn your cardstock 90 degrees clockwise. Score every inch on every odd row (1 inch, 3 inches, 5 inches, 7 inches, etc.); take your Scor-Tool from one line to the next, being careful not to score over that line. On every even row (2 inches, 4 inches, 6 inches, 8 inches, etc.), score every inch starting not from the left edge, but from the ½-inch line. Be careful to run your Scor-Tool only between the top and bottom line on that row. This will create the staggered look of brick when you are finished and have completed the pattern on every row. Turn paper 90 degrees and do the long vertical scores again. If you happened to go over your lines, this will correct it.

Tips, Tricks & Terms

- The general supplies needed to create projects are sharp scissors, a ruler and hot-glue gun.

- Embossing is the technique of creating a raised pattern on a piece of paper or cardstock.

- Debossing is the technique of creating an indented or depressed pattern onto a piece of paper of cardstock.

- Emboss or Deboss?—that is the question! Mix and match both embossed and debossed lines in your design to add even more depth. To emboss, score on the back, or wrong side, of the paper; to deboss, score on the front, or right side, of the paper.

- After embossing white core paper, gently rub along the embossed lines with a sanding block to reveal the paper's white core. You can also use this technique to sand the bumps created with the Scor-Bug tool.

- Made a mistake and scored the wrong side of the paper? Don't worry! Place the paper with the ridge side up on the same measurement on your Scor-Pal and re-emboss to remove the score line.

- For added effect, sponge ink or apply some metallic rub-on paint over your embossed lines to create a perfect backdrop for masculine cards and creations.

- When using the Scor-Bug, it is best to move the paper down from the top fence. This leaves you room to run off the paper at the top of the embossing motion.

- When scoring thinner papers, make sure to apply light pressure as pressing too hard can cut paper instead of scoring it.

- Make sure to cut straight lines or use a paper trimmer when creating a piece that will be scored; having straight edges creates an even base to score on.

- Burnishing scored lines can give a nice, crisp folded edge providing a more professional look when making boxes or folds.

- After adhering Scor-Tape to a piece, don't remove remaining paper backing to expose adhesive until it's time to adhere pieces together.

How to Read Templates, Patterns & Legends

Templates, patterns and their accompanying legends make creating complicated projects a breeze. This section will be your guide to understanding these elements and how they will be used in this book.

Legends are the key to all information illustrated in a template or pattern. Each template or pattern in this book will include a legend that contains all the symbols and markings used for that particular project. This Master Template Legend shows all symbols and markings that will be used within this book.

Templates in this book will illustrate dimensions along with instructions on how to score, fold and cut to create a project. These guides are presented on a smaller scale than what the finished project will be. When working with templates, try drawing the dimensions of the template out onto a scrap piece of paper before using the material your finished piece will be made from. This will give you a chance to practice creating your project before using more expensive materials.

Patterns in this book differ from templates because they are to scale, meaning the pattern is the exact size needed to create the project. In the same manner as a template, try tracing or using a copy machine to print a pattern onto scrap paper first to practice making the project.

Template Legend

· – · · – ·	Score line, mountain fold
– – –	Score line, valley fold
– – –	Score an embossed line, do not fold
——	Placement
——	Cutting line
——	Pencil line
▌ or ▬	Mark here
▬	Align at 6" Scor-Pal line
⌐	Corner post location
▢	Outside/right side
▨	Cut and remove
◠	Punch half circle
●	Punch hole
▭	Die cut or flap placement
	Scor-Tape placement (on inside/wrong side)
▬	Scor-Tape placement (on outside/right side)

Box Basics

Making boxes the exact size for a gift is as easy as following a few simple formulas. In this section you will learn simple ways to figure paper size and create single- and double-thickness boxes.

Boxes With Single-Thickness Walls

A box created with single-thickness walls simply means the walls of the box are made with just one layer of paper or cardstock. This is the perfect type of box to create for lightweight gifts. In order for the single-thickness box lid to fit over the bottom of the box, it needs to be a little larger. To achieve this, ⅛ inch is added to the overall measurement in the formula for the box lid. If using thinner paper and a tighter fit is desired, add ¹⁄₁₆ inch to the box-lid measurement instead of ⅛ inch.

Square Boxes

The following formulas show what size paper is needed to create a box that will be 4 x 4 x 2 inches.

Box Bottom Formula

Side + width + side = width of paper needed

Side + length + side = length of paper needed

Insert the numbers

2 inches + 4 inches + 2 inches = 8 inches

2 inches + 4 inches + 2 inches = 8 inches

The piece of paper needed to create a bottom for a 4 x 4 x 2-inch square box with single-thickness walls will be 8 x 8 inches.

Box Lid Formula

Side + width + side + ⅛ inch = width of paper needed

Side + length + side + ⅛ inch = length of paper needed

Insert the numbers

2 inches + 4 inches + 2 inches + ⅛ inch = 8⅛ inches

2 inches + 4 inches + 2 inches + ⅛ inch = 8⅛ inches

The piece of paper needed to create a lid for a 4 x 4 x 2-inch square box with single-thickness walls will be 8⅛ x 8⅛ inches.

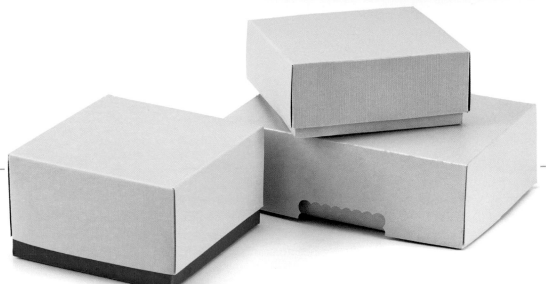

Rectangular Boxes

The following formulas show what size paper is needed to create a box that will be 4 x 6 x 2 inches in size.

Box Bottom Formula

Side + width + side = width of paper needed

Side + length + side = length of paper needed

Insert the numbers

2 inches + 4 inches + 2 inches = 8 inches

2 inches + 6 inches + 2 inches = 10 inches

The piece of paper needed to create a bottom for a 4 x 6 x 2-inch rectangle box with single-thickness walls will be 8 x 10 inches.

Box Lid Formula

Side + width + side + ⅛ inch = width of paper needed

Side + length + side + ⅛ inch = length of paper needed

Insert the numbers

2 inches + 4 inches + 2 inches + ⅛ inch = 8⅛ inches

2 inches + 6 inches + 2 inches + ⅛ inch = 10⅛ inches

The piece of paper needed to create a lid for a 4 x 6 x 2-inch rectangle box with single-thickness walls will be 8⅛ x 10⅛ inches.

Assembly Instructions for Boxes With Single-Thickness Walls

When making square boxes, you will always be working with a square piece of paper, and when making rectangle boxes, you will always be working with a rectangular piece of paper. If the sides of a box lid completely cover the box bottom, punch a half circle at the bottom edge of two of the lid sides. This will help when removing the lid from the box (Photo 1).

Referring to templates, score each side separately. With one edge of paper at top fence, score at 2 inches (Photo 2); rotate paper to the right and score at 2 inches; rotate paper to the right and score at 2 inches; rotate paper to the right and score at 2 inches (Photo 3). Refer to templates for cutting guidelines and Scor-Tape placement. Referring to photos, fold and assemble box (Photo 4). **Note:** *Scoring instructions are the same for both the box lid and bottom.*

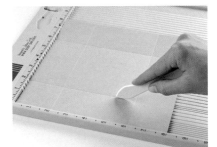

[Photo 1]

[Photo 2]

[Photo 3]

[Photo 4]

Boxes With Double-Thickness Walls

A box with double-thickness walls means the walls of the box are made with two layers of paper or cardstock. This kind of box will have a more finished appearance and is a little sturdier than a box with single-thickness walls. In the formula for the box lid, $\frac{3}{16}$ inch has been added to the overall measurement to ensure a good fit over the bottom of the box. *Note: The walls of these boxes are shorter than the single-thickness box walls so that a piece of paper or cardstock smaller than 12 x 12 inches can be used.*

Square Boxes

The following formulas show what size paper is needed to create a box that will be 4 x 4 x 1½ inches in size.

Box Bottom Formula

Side + side + width + side + side = width of paper needed

Side + side + length + side + side = length of paper needed

Insert the numbers

1½ inches + 1½ inches + 4 inches + 1½ inches + 1½ inches = 10 inches

1½ inches + 1½ inches + 4 inches + 1½ inches + 1½ inches = 10 inches

The piece of paper needed to create a bottom for a 4 x 4 x 1½-inch square box with double-thickness walls will be 10 x 10 inches.

Box Lid Formula

Side + side+ width + side + side + $\frac{3}{16}$ inch = width of paper needed

Side + side + length + side + side + $\frac{3}{16}$ inch = length of paper needed

Insert the numbers

1½ inches + 1½ inches + 4 inches + 1½ inches + 1½ inches + $\frac{3}{16}$ inch = $10\frac{3}{16}$ inches

1½ inches + 1½ inches + 4 inches + 1½ inches + 1½ inches + $\frac{3}{16}$ inch = $10\frac{3}{16}$ inches

The piece of paper needed to create a lid for a 4 x 4 x 1½-inch square box with double-thickness walls will be $10\frac{3}{16}$ x $10\frac{3}{16}$ inches.

Rectangle Boxes

The following formulas show what size paper is needed to create a box that will be 3 x 5 x 1½ inches in size.

Box Bottom Formula

Side + side + width + side + side = width of paper needed

Side + side + length + side + side = length of paper needed

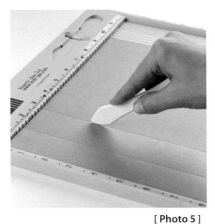

[Photo 5]

[Photo 6]

[Photo 7]

Insert the numbers

1½ inches + 1½ inches + 3 inches + 1½ inches + 1½ inches = 9 inches

1½ inches + 1½ inches + 5 inches + 1½ inches + 1½ inches = 11 inches

The piece of paper needed to create a bottom for a 3 x 5 x 1½-inch rectangle box with double-thickness walls will be 9 x 11 inches.

Box Lid Formula

Side + side + width + side + side + ³⁄₁₆ inch = width of paper needed

Side + side + length + side + side + ³⁄₁₆ inch = length of paper needed

Insert the numbers

1½ inches + 1½ inches + 3 inches + 1½ inches + 1½ inches + ³⁄₁₆ inch = 9³⁄₁₆ inches

1½ inches + 1½ inches + 5 inches + 1½ inches + 1½ inches + ³⁄₁₆ inch = 11³⁄₁₆ inches

[Photo 8]

The piece of paper needed to create the lid for a 3 x 5 x 1½-inch rectangle box with double-thickness wall will be 9³⁄₁₆ x 11³⁄₁₆.

Assembly Instructions for Boxes With Double-Thickness Walls

When making square boxes, you will always be working with a square piece of paper or cardstock, and when making rectangular boxes, you will always be working with a rectangular piece of paper or cardstock.

Referring to templates, score each side separately. With one edge of paper at top fence, score at 1½ inches and 3 inches (Photo 5); rotate paper to the right and score at 1½ inches and 3 inches; rotate to the right and score at 1½ inches and 3 inches; rotate to the right and score at 1½ inches and 3 inches (Photo 6). Refer to templates for cutting guidelines and Scor-Tape placement. Referring to photos, fold and assemble box (Photos 7–9). **Note:** *Scoring instructions are the same for both the box lid and bottom.*

[Photo 9]

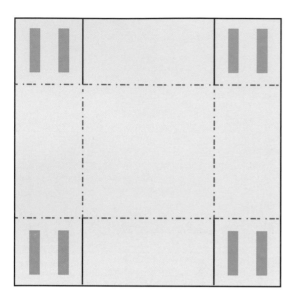

Box Basics
Single-Thickness Square Box Template

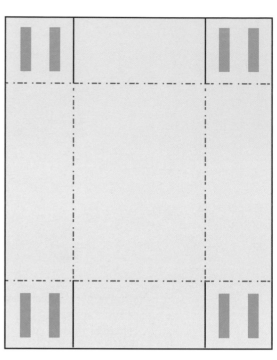

Box Basics
Single-Thickness Rectangular Box Template

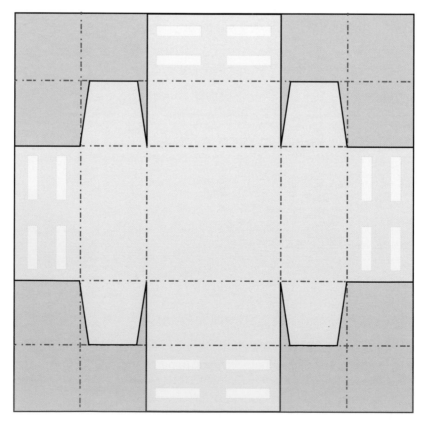

Box Basics
Double-Thickness Square Box Template

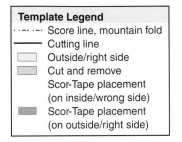

Template Legend
- ·—·—·— Score line, mountain fold
- —— Cutting line
- ☐ Outside/right side
- ▨ Cut and remove
- ☐ Scor-Tape placement (on inside/wrong side)
- ▪ Scor-Tape placement (on outside/right side)

Box Basics
Double-Thickness Rectangular Box Template

Basic Rosettes

By **Tami Mayberry**

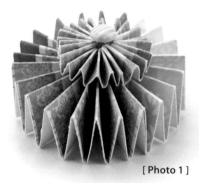

[Photo 1]

Rosettes have become a trendy item currently found on paper-craft projects of all types. Rosettes are easy to make and are all created with the same basic technique. A strip of paper is cut, scored in even intervals, the ends connected to form a circle and finally the center is pressed down and secured in place.

While rosettes can be purchased premade or created with dies, the most versatile tool for this type of embellishment is the Scor-Pal. By using the Scor-Pal to create rosettes, the project is not limited to a specific color or pattern as with premade embellishments; unlike dies, when using the Scor-Pal the thickness, fullness and diameter can all be changed by adjusting various measurements (shown below).

Thickness

The wider the distance between scores, the taller the rosette will be.

Paper is 1 x 36 inches, scored every ¾ inch (Photo 1).

Smaller rosette is ½ x 12 inches, scored every ¼ inch.

Fullness

[Photo 2]

The longer the paper strip, the fuller the rosette. If longer paper is needed, adhere two pieces together end to end.

Paper is 1 x 48 inches long, scored every ½ inch (Photo 2).

Diameter

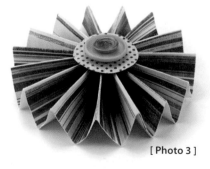

[Photo 3]

The wider the paper strip, the larger the diameter of the rosette will be. Finished rosettes will be approximately two times in diameter to the width of the strip.

Paper is 2 x 36 inches long, scored every inch. Rosette is 4 inches wide (Photo 3).

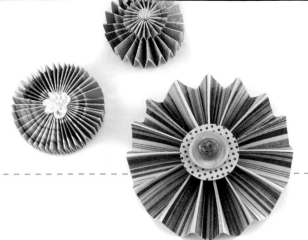

Rosettes Technique

1. Cut a strip of printed paper, or cardstock of choice, to ¾ x 10 inches.

2. Using the Scor-Pal, score every ½ inch across length of cut paper. Turn scored paper over. Shift paper to the ¼-inch mark on the Scor-Pal and score again every ½ inch (Photo 4). Accordion-fold piece (Photo 5).

3. Attach ends of accordion-folded paper using Scor-Tape (Photo 6). Make a circle of hot glue on the Stay Put Craft Mat and lower the tight rosette into the hot glue. Push center of folded paper down (Photo 7).

4. Adhere a small circle of paper or cardstock to center back and front of rosette to secure in place (Photo 8). Embellish as desired. ***Note:*** *Some projects will list what size circle should be adhered to front and back of rosette.*

When creating rosettes, it is critical to use a very strong adhesive. Scor-Tape works wonderfully for attaching the ends of the paper strip, as the widths are the same as the typical scored sections. When securing the center, the most stable adhesive option is the use of hot glue. This becomes even more convenient when used with the Stay Put Craft Mat. The Stay Put Craft Mat is nonstick and heat resistant. Therefore, a drop of hot glue can be placed on the mat and the rosette center quickly pressed down onto it. Hold the embellishment in place until dry, and then simply peel off and add to the desired project.

> *If you are making a series of rosettes from the same paper, score the whole sheet of paper first, then cut the necessary widths of paper.*
> Tip

[Photo 5]

[Photo 6]

[Photo 7]

[Photo 4]

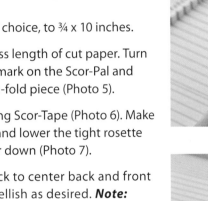

[Photo 8]

Victorian Drawers

Design by **Brenda Quintana**

Materials
› Scor-Pal
› Scor-Tape
› Red cardstock
› Assorted red/pink printed papers
› Cardboard
› Dye ink pads: red, dark brown
› Silver Victorian brads: 2 large, 2 medium
› Key and lock set
› Silver crown
› Paper roses
› Scrap cream lace
› 2 x 3-inch scallop oval mirror
› Top Note die (#113463)
› Die-cutting machine
› Paper piercer
› Adhesive foam dots
› Adhesive dots

[Photo 1]

[Photo 2]

[Photo 3]

[Photo 4]

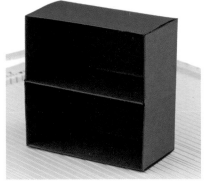

[Photo 5]

Project note: Decorate drawers with paper roses, lace, crown and key and lock set; ink edges, printed papers, cardstock and paper roses dark brown and red as desired. Refer to Box Basics technique section when assembling drawer base and drawers. When assembling pieces, if needed, trim edges of scored pieces for a better fit.

Pieces to Cut

Drawer Base: 12 x 12-inch cardstock

Drawer Shelf: 8 x 8-inch cardstock

Square Drawers: Two 9⅜ x 9⅜-inch pink floral printed paper

Rectangular Drawer: 11⅜ x 9⅜-inch red dot paper

Drawer Back: 4 x 6¾-inch cardstock

Drawer Back Support: 3 x 6-inch cardboard

Scoring & Assembling

Drawer Base & Shelf

1. With one edge of Drawer Base piece at top fence, score mountain folds at 2-inch, 4-inch, 8-inch and 10-inch marks.

2. Rotate piece and repeat scoring in the same manner. Draw a 2-inch-long line at 6-inch point. Repeat on opposite side of piece.

3. Refer to Drawer Base template for cutting instructions and Scor-Tape placement. Fold along score lines; set aside.

4. With one edge of Drawer Shelf piece at top fence, score a valley fold at 2-inch and 6-inch marks. Score a mountain fold at 4-inch mark.

5. Rotate piece; with edge at top fence, score at 2-inch and 6-inch marks.

6. Refer to Drawer Shelf template for cutting instructions. Fold along score lines; set aside.

Drawer Base & Shelf Assembly

1. Referring to photo and with Drawer Base piece inside facing up on work surface, fold tabs in and edge up on one side; adhere in place with Scor-Tape. Repeat with remaining edge (Photos 1 and 2).

2. Referring to photos, fold Drawer Shelf into shelf shape (Photo 3).

3. Insert Drawer Shelf piece into Drawer Base (Photo 4).

4. Fold side tabs of Drawer Base in and adhere in place (Photo 5).

5. Adhere Drawer Back Support to back of drawer base aligning bottom edges.

6. Die-cut top short edge of Drawer Back piece. Adhere over Drawer Back Support piece aligning bottom edges.

7. Die-cut a piece from red dot paper; trim as needed and adhere as shown. Adhere mirror as shown using foam dots and adhesive dots.

Rectangular & Square Drawers

1. With long edge of Rectangular Drawer piece at top fence, score mountain folds at 1⅞-inch and 3¾-inch marks; repeat on each side of piece. ***Note:*** *To score 1⅞-inch lines, either use a ruler to measure and trace lines onto piece and align line with a scoring line on Scor-Pal or align edge of paper with first score line on Scor-Pal and score at 2-inch mark.*

2. Refer to Rectangular Drawer template for cutting instructions and Scor-Tape placement. Fold along score lines, set aside.

3. In the same manner, score Square Drawer pieces at 1⅞-inch and 3¾-inch marks on each side.

4. Refer to Square Drawer template for cutting instructions and Scor-Tape placement. Fold along score lines; set aside.

Rectangular & Square Drawers Assembly

1. Refer to Box Basics techniques when assembling both the rectangle drawer and square drawers.

2. Pierce a hole through center front of each square drawer and insert large brad for drawer pull. Pierce two holes through front of rectangular drawer as shown; insert medium brads for drawer pull. ◄

Sources: *Scor-Pal and Scor-Tape from Scor-Pal Products; cardstock from Bazzill Basics Paper Inc.; dye ink pads, Victorian brads, crown and die from Stampin' Up!; Tim Holtz Locket Keys key and lock set from Ranger Industries Inc.; paper roses from Prima Marketing Inc.*

Try making four square drawers or two rectangular drawers for this set of drawers for a different look.

Tip

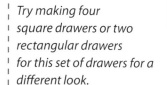

Template Legend

- ·—·—· Score line, mountain fold
- – – – Score line, valley fold
- ——— Cutting line
- ——— Pencil line
- ▢ Outside/right side
- ▢ Cut and remove
- ▢ Scor-Tape placement (on inside/wrong side)
- ▮ Scor-Tape placement (on outside/right side)

9³/₈"

9³/₈"

1⁷/₈" 1⁷/₈" 1⁷/₈" 1⁷/₈" 1⁷/₈"

Victorian Drawers
Square Drawer Template

12"

12"

2" 2" 2" 2" 2" 2"

} ¹/₈"

2" 2" 4"

Victorian Drawers
Drawer Base Template

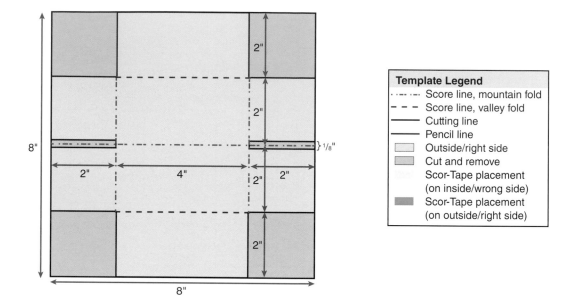

Template Legend

·—·—· Score line, mountain fold
- - - Score line, valley fold
—— Cutting line
—— Pencil line
Outside/right side
Cut and remove
Scor-Tape placement
(on inside/wrong side)
Scor-Tape placement
(on outside/right side)

Victorian Drawers
Drawer Shelf Template

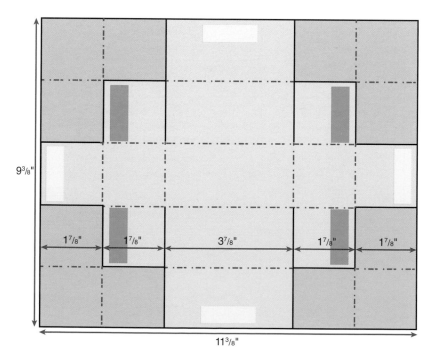

Victorian Drawers
Rectangular Drawer Template

Cake Gift Box

Design by **Tami Mayberry**

Materials
› Scor-Pal
› Scor-Tape
› Cardstock: ivory, pink
› Clear iridescent glitter spray
› 1 yard ¼-inch-wide pink double-loop ribbon
› White self-adhesive pearls: medium, mini
› Pink birthday candle
› Double Scallop Border die
› Die-cutting machine
› Paper trimmer with scalloped edge blade
› Hot-glue gun
› Adhesive squares

Project note: *Refer to Box Basics technique section when assembling boxes and lids. Embellish assembled boxes as desired using pearls, glitter spray, ribbon and candle. Several pieces of ivory cardstock will be used for scalloped borders; create enough border pieces to decorate boxes as desired. Cut all pink cardstock pieces using paper trimmer with a scalloped edge blade.*

Pieces to Cut

Bottom Box: 8 x 8-inch ivory cardstock

Top Box: 7 x 7-inch ivory cardstock

Base Panel: 5 x 5-inch pink cardstock

Bottom Box Lid: 6⅛ x 6⅛-inch pink cardstock

Bottom Lid Topper: 5¼ x 5¼-inch pink cardstock

Top Box Lid: 5⅛ x 5⅛-inch pink cardstock

Top Lid Topper: 4¼ x 4¼-inch pink cardstock

Rosette: Two 12 x ¾-inch pink cardstock

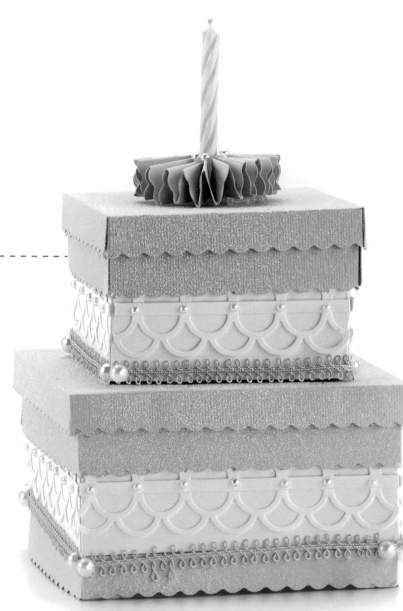

Scoring & Assembling

Boxes

1. Score Bottom Box piece at 2-inch mark on all sides.

2. Refer to Bottom Box Template for cutting instructions and Scor-Tape placement. Assemble box.

3. Repeat steps 1–2 for Top Box piece referring to Top Box Template.

Base & Lids

1. Score Base Panel piece at ½-inch mark on all sides.

2. Refer to Base Panel Template for cutting instructions and Scor-Tape placement. Assemble base.

3. Repeat steps 1–2 for remaining lid and lid topper pieces referring to corresponding templates for scoring measurements, cutting instructions and Scor-Tape placement.

Assembly

Project note: *Refer to photo throughout assembly.*

1. Adhere Base Panel to bottom of Bottom Box.

2. Adhere Bottom Lid Topper over Bottom Box Lid. Adhere bottom of Top Box to top of Bottom Lid Topper.

3. Adhere Top Lid Topper over Top Box Lid.

4. Referring to Basic Rosettes technique, create a rosette from two Rosette pieces. Adhere to top of Top Lid Topper.

5. Stack completed pieces together creating a gift box. ❮

Sources: *Scor-Pal and Scor-Tape from Scor-Pal Products; glitter spray from Krylon; ribbon from Creative Impressions Inc.; self-adhesive pearls from Want2Scrap; die from My Favorite Things; paper trimmer from Fiskars; adhesive squares from GlueArts.*

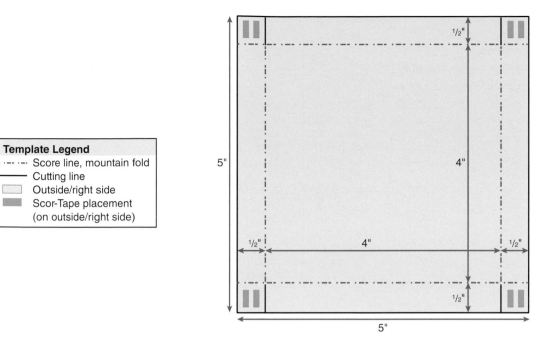

Template Legend
- ·–·–·– Score line, mountain fold
- —— Cutting line
- ▱ Outside/right side
- ▰ Scor-Tape placement (on outside/right side)

5"

1/2"

4"

1/2" 4" 1/2"

1/2"

5"

Cake Gift Box
Base Panel Template

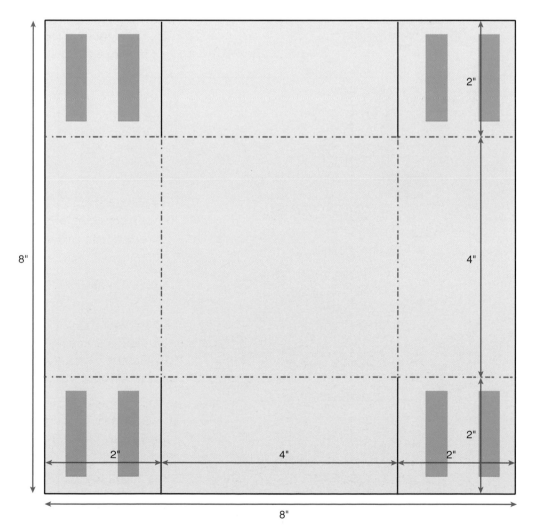

8"

2"

4"

2"

2"

2" 4" 2" 2"

8"

Cake Gift Box
Bottom Box Template

The Ultimate Guide to Crafting With Scor-Pal [**29**]

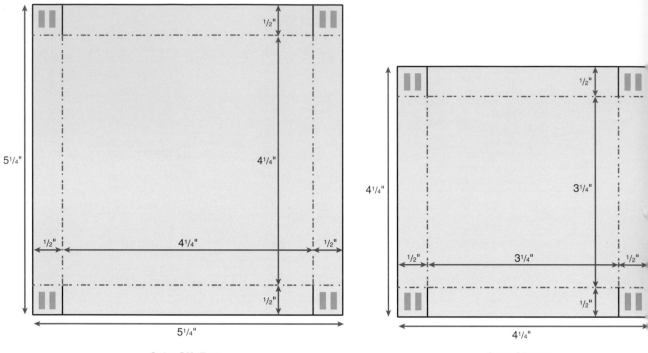

Cake Gift Box
Bottom Lid Topper Template

Cake Gift Box
Top Lid Topper Template

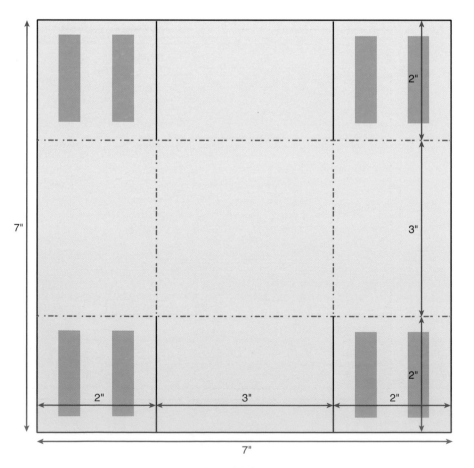

Cake Gift Box
Top Box Template

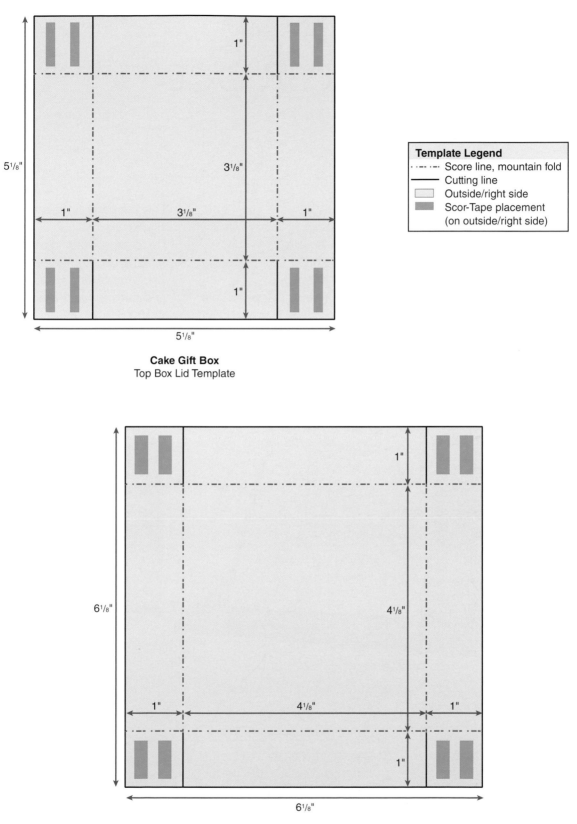

Template Legend
- ·—·· Score line, mountain fold
- —— Cutting line
- ☐ Outside/right side
- ▨ Scor-Tape placement (on outside/right side)

Cake Gift Box
Top Box Lid Template

Cake Gift Box
Bottom Box Lid Template

ABC Desk Set

Designs by **Julie Koerber**

Materials

- › Scor-Pal
- › Scor-Tape
- › Ivory cardstock
- › An ABC Primer Collection printed papers
- › An ABC Primer chipboard die cuts: 1, 2
- › Plain chipboard
- › 5 packs 3-inch sticky notes
- › An ABC Primer stamp sets: 1, 2
- › Dye ink pads: light brown, black, red
- › Decorative brad
- › 4 inches ⅝-inch-wide ruler printed ribbon
- › Die-cutting machine
- › Craft knife
- › Ruler
- › 3-D adhesive squares

[Photo 1]

[Photo 1B]

[Photo 2]

Project note: Refer to Box Basics technique section when assembling cubby and drawer. Embellish assembled pieces with chipboard die cuts, ribbon and brad as desired.

Pieces to Cut
Pencil Holder: 11 x 12-inch Building Blocks paper

Pencil Holder Bottom Pattern: 2 x 2¾-inch cardstock

Base: Two 5 x 8-inch, one from plain chipboard, one from The Three R's paper

Calendar Easel: 4 x 9-inch The Three R's paper

Calendar Easel Stand: 2½ x 5-inch The Three R's paper

Calendar Pages: 12 (3¾ x 4½-inch) cardstock

Calendar Mats: 12 (4 x 4¾-inch) desired printed papers

Cubby: 11¾ x 11¾-inch Calico Kids paper

Drawer: 8⅛ x 8⅛-inch School Days paper

Drawer Divider: 3⅛ x 5½-inch Games and Playtime paper

Cubby Shelf Insert: 4¼ x 9-inch Alphabet Soup paper

Sticky Note Covers: Five 3⅛ x 6½-inch desired printed papers

Scoring & Assembling
Pencil Holder
Project note: Do not score with very tip of scoring tool—this may crack paper and show its core.

1. Referring to Pencil Holder Template and with long edge of Pencil Holder piece right side up at top fence, score a mountain fold at 6-inch mark. Turn piece over and score valley folds at 1-inch and 11-inch marks.

2. With short edge of Pencil Holder piece at top fence, score at 2-inch, 4¾-inch, 6¾-inch and 9½-inch marks.

3. Refer to Pencil Holder Template for cutting instructions and Scor-Tape placement.

4. Remove backing from Scor-Tape on 5 x 9½-inch section. Fold piece in half at 6-inch scored line and adhere wrong sides together. *Note: Do not remove backing on any other section of Scor-Tape at this time.*

5. Referring to Folded Pencil Holder Template and with fold at top fence, line up previously scored lines. Rescore over scored lines.

6. Refer to Folded Pencil Holder Template for additional Scor-Tape placement on 1½ x 5-inch flap. Fold at scored lines and adhere 1½-inch flap to inside of opposite 2-inch section, creating pencil holder box (Photo 1). *Note: Do not adhere bottom flaps together.*

7. Fold inside bottom flaps in and adhere, creating bottom of pencil holder; do not adhere outer bottom flaps (Photo 1B).

8. Referring to Base Template for placement, place Pencil Holder Bottom Pattern piece onto paper Base piece. Draw around pattern using pencil on wrong side of paper Base piece. Cut out using craft knife (Photo 2). *Note: Adhere cutout piece to inside bottom of pencil holder.*

9. Place paper Base piece over chipboard Base piece, aligning edges. Using a pencil, trace cutout opening onto chipboard piece. Remove paper Base piece.

10. Align bottom of pencil holder with pencil marks from step 9. Adhere bottom flaps of Pencil Holder piece to chipboard Base trim edges of flaps as needed if they extend past base edges (Photo 3). *Note: Add additional Scor-Tape as needed to flaps.*

11. Using Scor-Tape as needed, place and adhere paper Base piece over chipboard Base piece (Photo 4).

12. Ink edges of Base piece black.

Calendar
1. With long edge of Calendar Easel piece right side up at top fence, score a mountain fold at 4-inch mark. Turn paper over and score a valley fold at 8-inch mark.

2. Refer to Calendar Easel Template for Scor-Tape placement. Adhere two 4-inch sections together; do not adhere 1-inch flap (Photo 5).

3. With long edge of Calendar Easel Stand piece right side up at top fence, score a mountain fold at 2½-inch mark.

4. Using pencil and ruler and referring to Easel Stand Template, lightly draw lines from bottom

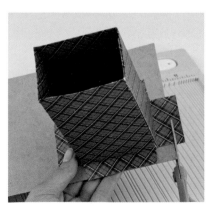

[Photo 3]

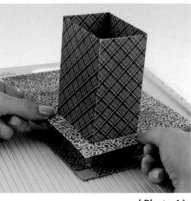

[Photo 4]

[Photo 5]

[Photo 6]

[Photo 7]

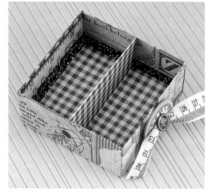

[Photo 8]

[Photo 9]

corners of piece to top point of scored line. Align these drawn lines to a groove on Scor-Pal and score valley fold lines. Fold these scored lines inward; unfold.

5. Refer to Easel Stand Template for Scor-Tape placement.

6. Remove tape backing on inside triangle area. Fold and adhere this section to matching triangle section on other side of 2½-inch scored line, creating easel stand (Photo 6).

7. Referring to Calendar Easel Template for placement, adhere easel stand to back of Calendar Easel piece (Photo 7).

8. Refer to Base Template for Calendar Easel placement and adhere 1-inch flap of Calendar Easel piece to Base piece. Adhere chipboard ruler piece along bottom edge of Calendar Easel piece; this piece will hold Calendar Pages Pieces in place when they are set on the easel.

9. Using ruler as a guide, stamp dates onto Calendar Page pieces. Use desired stamps to decorate top edges of Calendar Page pieces.

10. Adhere Calendar Page pieces to Calendar Mat pieces.

Organizing Cubby
Project note: *Sticky notes can come in a variety of thicknesses; peel off*

layers to correspond with Sticky Note Cover size.

1. With one edge of Cubby piece at top fence, score at 1-inch, 4¼-inch, 7½-inch and 10¾-inch marks. Rotate piece 90 degrees and repeat scoring instructions.

2. Refer to Cubby Template for cutting instructions and Scor-Tape placement.

3. Assemble cubby, making sure to fold down and adhere 1-inch tabs last.

4. With one edge of Drawer piece at top fence, score at 1-inch and 2½-inch marks. Rotate and repeat on all sides.

5. Refer to Drawer Template for cutting instructions and Scor-Tape placement.

6. Assemble drawer, making sure to fold down and adhere 1-inch tabs last.

7. With long edge of Drawer Divider piece right side up at top fence, score a mountain fold at 2¾-inch mark. Turn piece over and score valley folds at 1½-inch and 4-inch marks.

8. Refer to Drawer Divider Template for Scor-Tape placement.

9. Adhere 1¼-inch sections together; insert and adhere into drawer (Photo 8).

10. With long edge of Cubby Shelf Insert piece wrong side up at top fence, score at 4½-inch mark. Turn piece over and score at 1½-inch and 7½-inch marks.

11. With short edge of piece right side up at top fence, score at ½-inch and 3¾-inch marks.

12. Refer to Cubby Shelf Insert Template for cutting instructions and Scor-Tape placement.

13. Adhere 3-inch sections of Cubby Shelf Insert piece together, leaving side flaps and 1½-inch flaps on either side unadhered and folded out.

14. Before adhering Cubby Shelf Insert into Cubby, check to ensure Drawer piece will fit snugly underneath shelf. Adhere shelf in place (Photo 9).

15. With long edge of a Sticky Note Cover piece at top edge of Scor-Pal and left edge of piece at middle of ⅞-inch mark, score at 4-inch mark. Move left edge of piece to center of ⅝-inch mark and score at 4-inch mark.

16. Adhere one large section of Sticky Note Cover to back of sticky note pack aligning spine of sticky note with closest scored line. Fold over front of sticky note pack, creating a front cover. Repeat with remaining sticky notes.

17. Place drawer and covered sticky notes into cubby. ❰

Sources: *Scor-Pal and Scor-Tape from Scor-Pal Products; printed paper collection, chipboard die cuts and stamp sets from Graphic 45; decorative brad from Stampin' Up!; ribbon from The Paper Studio; 3-D adhesive squares from GlueArts.*

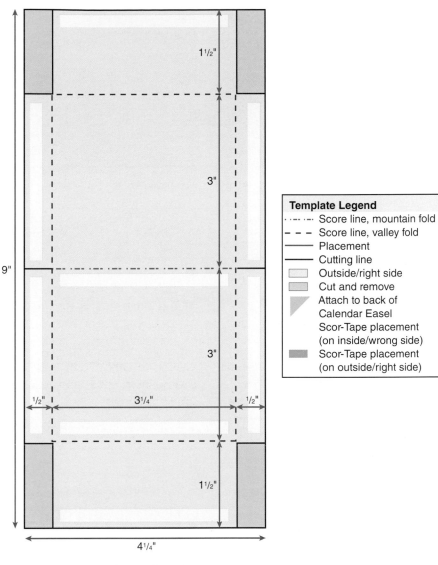

Template Legend
·–··–··–	Score line, mountain fold
– – –	Score line, valley fold
———	Placement
———	Cutting line
▭	Outside/right side
▨	Cut and remove
◥	Attach to back of Calendar Easel
	Scor-Tape placement (on inside/wrong side)
▨	Scor-Tape placement (on outside/right side)

ABC Desk Calendar
Cubby Shelf Insert Template

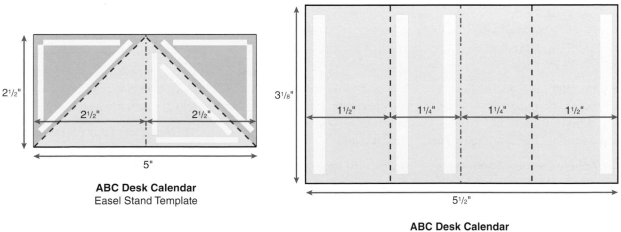

ABC Desk Calendar
Easel Stand Template

ABC Desk Calendar
Drawer Divider Template

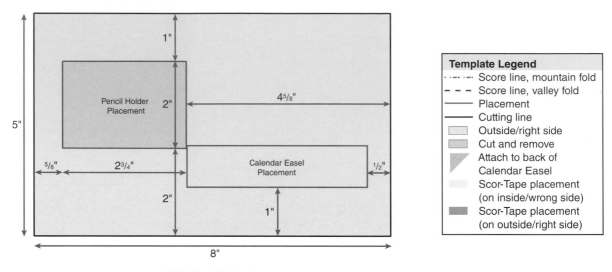

ABC Desk Calendar
Base Template

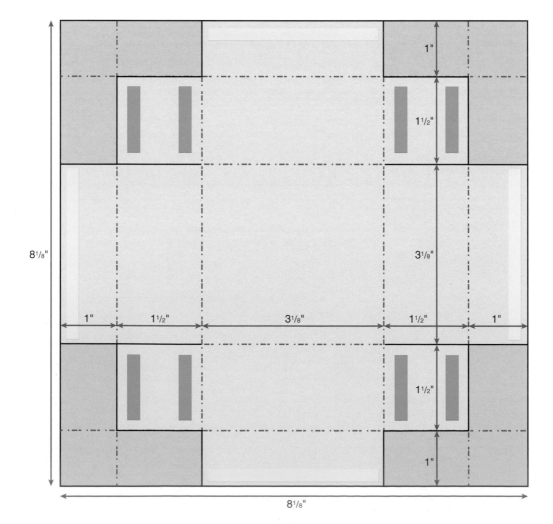

ABC Desk Calendar
Drawer Template

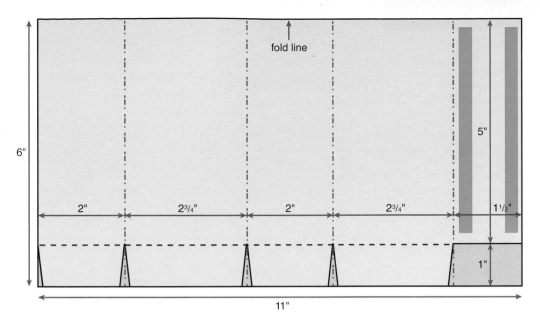

ABC Desk Calendar
Folded Pencil Holder Template

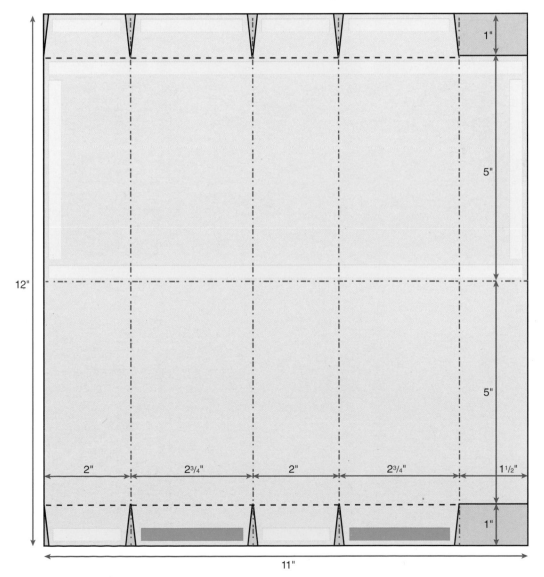

ABC Desk Calendar
Pencil Holder Template

Template Legend

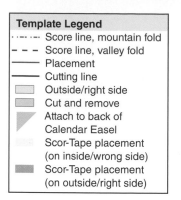

- ·–··–· Score line, mountain fold
- – – – Score line, valley fold
- —— Placement
- —— Cutting line
- ▢ Outside/right side
- ▨ Cut and remove
- ◪ Attach to back of Calendar Easel
- ▢ Scor-Tape placement (on inside/wrong side)
- ▨ Scor-Tape placement (on outside/right side)

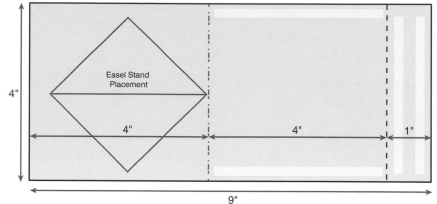

Easel Stand Placement

4"

4"

4"

1"

9"

ABC Desk Calendar
Calendar Easel Template

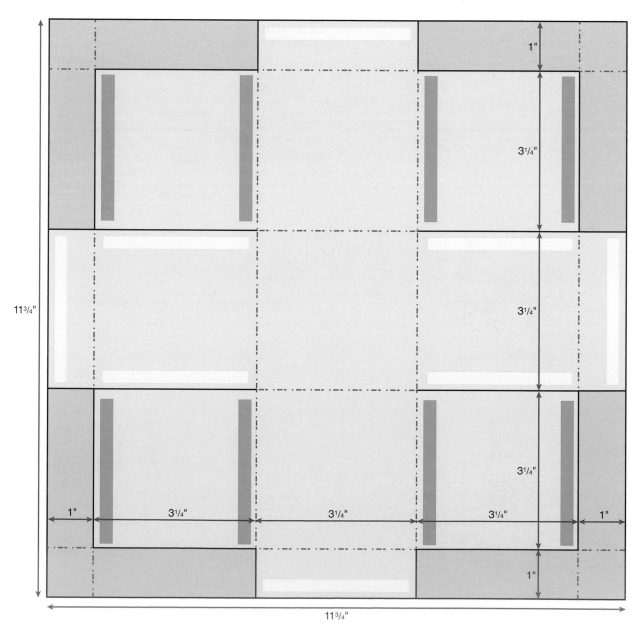

1"

3¼"

3¼"

3¼"

11¾"

1"   3¼"   3¼"   3¼"   3¼"   1"

1"

11¾"

ABC Desk Calendar
Cubby Template

Way to Go

Design by **Kim Hughes**

Pieces to Cut

Card Base: 8½ x 4¼-inch aqua cardstock

Panel: 4 x 4-inch dark aqua cardstock

Star: 4 x 4-inch dark yellow cardstock

Sentiment Banner: 4 x ¾-inch white cardstock

Scoring & Assembling

1. With long edge of Card Base at top fence, score a line at 4¼-inch mark. Fold at scored line creating a 4¼ x 4¼-inch card.

2. Referring to photo, with an edge of Panel piece at top fence, score three lines ¼ inch apart. Rotate right and repeat scoring instructions. Repeat until three lines have been scored on each side of piece. Adhere to card front.

3. Stamp sentiment centered onto Sentiment Banner piece.

4. With long edge of Sentiment Banner piece at top fence, score lines at ¾-inch, 1-inch, 3-inch and 3¼-inch marks. Cut a V-notch at each end of banner. Referring to photo, fold at scored lines and attach to card front using foam squares.

Try alternating between embossed and debossed lines. Tip

5. Cut or punch a star from Star piece.

6. Referring to photo, score lines from points and corners on star to center. Fold slightly at scored lines to give star a dimensional look. Attach to card front using foam squares. ❮

Sources: *Scor-Pal and Scor-Tape from Scor-Pal Products; cardstock from Bazzill Basics Paper Inc.; stamp set from Paper Smooches; dye ink pad from Imagine Crafts/Tsukineko; punch from Uchida of America Corp.; foam squares from Therm O Web Inc.*

Materials

› Scor-Pal
› Scor-Tape
› Cardstock: aqua, dark aqua, dark yellow, white
› Sentiment Sampler stamp set
› Black dye ink pad
› Giga Star punch
› Adhesive foam squares

You Inspire Me Gatefold Card

Design by **Julie Koerber**

Materials
› Scor-Pal
› Scor-Bug
› Scor-Tape
› Ivory smooth cardstock
› Printed papers: Old School Curriculum, red dot, red kraft
› Stamps: Feminine Form, Sweet Violets set
› Dye ink pads: black, light brown distress
› Copic® markers: C00, C03, R20, R39, R59, Y21, Y23, YG13, YR0000
› Colorless Blender (0)
› 6½ inches ⅜-inch-wide two-tone red ribbon
› 7 inches ½-inch-wide cream crochet trim
› White self-adhesive pearls: 2 small, 1 medium
› Silver decorative brad
› Grand Labels One die templates (#LF-161)
› Grand Calibur™
› Sandpaper
› Craft sponge

Project note: Distress edges of cut pieces with sandpaper and light brown ink. Use self-adhesive pearls, ribbon and brad to embellish card front as desired.

Pieces to Cut
Card Base: 11 x 7-inch red kraft printed paper

Decorative Layers: Two 4 x 7½-inch Curriculum paper

Image Panel: 2 x 5⅝-inch cardstock

Image Mat: 2⅝ x 5¾-inch red dot

Sentiment: 2¾ x ½-inch cardstock

Scoring & Assembling
Card Base
1. With long edge of Card Base at top fence facedown, score mountain folds at 2¾-inch and 8¼-inch marks.

2. Fold in at scored lines, creating a 5½ x 7-inch gatefold card with two 2¾-inch-wide front panels.

Decorative Layers
1. Place one Decorative Layer piece onto Scor-Pal, aligning two opposite corners on 6-inch mark. Firmly hold piece in place and score, starting at 3-inch mark, then score at every inch and end at 9-inch mark.

2. Rotate piece so opposite corners are aligned at 6-inch mark. Score, starting at 3-inch mark, then score at every inch and end at 9-inch mark. Leave piece in place.

3. Using Scor-Bug (set to score dots), score piece every inch starting at 3½-inch mark and ending at 8½-inch mark.

4. Using largest Grand Labels One die template, die-cut a label from scored Decorative Layer piece. **Note:** *This will not produce a complete die-cut label.*

5. Repeat steps 1–4 with remaining Decorative Layer piece.

6. Adhere finished Decorative Layer pieces to front panels of card base.

Image Panel, Mat & Sentiment Panel
1. Using black ink, stamp image onto Image Panel.

2. With image panel facedown, score each edge at ⅛-inch mark.

3. Stamp image onto a scrap piece of cardstock. Color as shown using markers and Colorless Blender; cut out. Adhere over image on Image Panel.

4. Adhere Image Panel to Image Mat as shown. Wrap crochet trim around layered panel as shown; secure ends to back.

5. Referring to photo, adhere layered panel to left front panel making sure to apply Scor-Tape to back left side of layered panel only.

6. Using black ink, stamp sentiment onto Sentiment piece; stamp scroll frame around sentiment using light brown ink.

7. Cut a V-notch at one short edge of Sentiment piece. Adhere to card front as shown. ❮

Sources: Scor-Pal, Scor-Tape and Scor-Bug from Scor-Pal Products; Curriculum printed paper from Pink Paislee; Feminine Form stamp from Impression Obsession Inc.; Sweet Violets stamp set from Flourishes; black dye ink pad from Imagine Crafts/Tsukineko; light brown distress ink pad from Ranger Industries Inc.; markers and Colorless Blender from Imagination International Inc.; brad from Stampin' Up!; die templates and die-cutting machine from Spellbinders™ Paper Arts.

Rosette Christmas Trees

Designs by **Bonnie Szwalkiewicz**

Materials
› Scor-Pal
› Scor-Tape
› White cardstock
› Assorted printed papers
› Cardboard tube (from paper towels)
› Desired embellishments
› Punches: 1-inch circle, decorative-edge (optional)
› Hot-glue gun

Pieces to Cut

Project note: Measurements are listed from the base-size up. Cut pieces from desired printed papers.

Large Tree

Layer 1: Three 5 x 12-inch strips

Layer 2: Three 4½ x 12-inch strips

Layer 3: Three 4 x 12-inch strips

Layer 4: Three 3¾ x 12-inch strips

Layer 5: Three 3½ x 12-inch strips

Layer 6: Three 3¼ x 12-inch strips

Layer 7: Three 3 x 12-inch strips

Layer 8: Three 2¾ x 12-inch strips

Layer 9: Three 2½ x 12-inch strips

Layer 10: Three 2¼ x 12-inch strips

Layer 11: Two 2 x 12-inch strips

Layer 12: Two 1¾ x 12-inch strips

Layer 13: Two 1½ x 12-inch strips

Layer 14: One 1 x 12-inch strip

Star: One ¾ x 12-inch strip

Center Pieces: 27 (1-inch) circles

Small Trees

Layer 1: Three 2¾ x 12-inch strips

Layer 2: Three 2½ x 12-inch strips

Layer 3: Three 2¼ x 12-inch strips

Layer 4: Two 2 x 12-inch strips

Layer 5: Two 1¾ x 12-inch strips

Layer 6: Two 1½ x 12-inch strips

Layer 7: One 1 x 12-inch strip

Star: One ¾ x 12-inch strip

Scoring & Assembling

Rosette Layers

Project note: These instructions can be applied to both the large and small tree. Punch one long edge of each Layer strip with decorative-edge punch if desired.

1. With long edge of Layer 1 strip at top fence, score at ½-inch mark. Repeat with remaining two Layer 1 strips.

2. Adhere short edges of three Layer 1 strips, creating one long strip. Referring to Basic Rosettes technique, create a rosette from long scored strip. Using hot-glue gun, attach a Center Piece to center of each side of rosette.

3. Repeat steps 1 and 2 with remaining Layer strips. When finishing last Layer strip (1-inch-wide piece), only adhere a Center Piece to bottom center of piece.

4. When creating rosette from Star piece, do not adhere a Center Piece to this piece. Instead, secure with hot glue at center and desired embellishment.

Tree Assembly

1. Cover cardboard tube with printed paper and cut into 13 (¼-inch) pieces.

2. Starting with Layer 1 rosette, alternating rosette and spacers, center and hot glue each layer together, building a tree from bottom up.

3. Adhere bottom edge of Star rosette to tree as shown. ❰

Source: Scor-Pal and Scor-Tape from Scor-Pal Products.

Flexy Fold Card

Design by **Mindy Baxter**

[Photo 1]

[Photo 2]

[Photo 3]

Materials

› Scor-Pal
› Scor-Tape
› Cardstock: light blue, white smooth
› Country Drive printed papers: Daisy Field, Just Dandy
› Stamps: School Yard Fun set; Up, Up and Away
› Dye ink pads: black, brown
› Markers
› Paper flowers
› 18 inches ⅝-inch-wide yellow ribbon
› Turquoise self-adhesive gems
› Tilda Lace die
› Die-cutting machine
› Craft knife
› Adhesive foam tape

Project note: Inspiration for this project is from www.schnauzerama. org/files/Bendy_Fold_Card_Tutorial. pdf. Decorate card with ribbon, gems and paper flowers as desired.

Pieces to Cut

Card Base: 5½ x 4¼-inch light blue cardstock

Layer 1: 5⅜ x 4⅛-inch Daisy Field paper

Bottom Panel: 5½ x 2½-inch light blue cardstock

Layer 2: 4⅝ x 2⅜-inch Just Dandy paper

Top Panel: 5½ x 1¾-inch printed paper

Layer 3: 4⅝ x 1⅝-inch Daisy Field paper

Decorative Edge: 4½ x 1-inch white smooth cardstock

Image Panel: 3 x 4-inch white smooth cardstock

Sentiment Panel: 2 x 2-inch white smooth cardstock

Scoring & Assembling
Card Base

1. With long edge of Bottom Panel piece at top fence, score at ½-inch mark. Repeat with Top Panel piece (Photo 1).

2. Using provided Bottom Panel and Top Panel Patterns, use craft knife to cut tabs onto unscored short edge of pieces (Photo 2).

3. Adhere Layer 1 piece to Card Base piece, Layer 2 piece to Bottom Panel piece and Layer 3 to Top Panel piece. Die-cut one long edge of Decorative Edge piece using Tilda Lace die. Adhere to top inside edge of Top Panel piece.

4. Adhere ½-inch flap on Bottom Panel piece to left back of Card Base piece as shown (Photo 3).

5. Referring to Card Base Pattern and using a craft knife, cut a slit through Card Base piece (Photo 4).

Note: Use notch on Bottom Panel piece as a guide for length of slit.

6. Insert tab of Bottom Panel piece into slit on Card Base piece (Photo 5).

7. Adhere ½-inch flap on Top Panel piece to right back of Card Base piece.

8. Referring to Bottom Panel Pattern, cut a slit through Bottom Panel piece (Photo 6). *Note: Use notch on Top Panel piece as a guide for length of slit.*

9. Insert tab of Top Panel piece into slit on Bottom Panel piece.

Image & Sentiment Panel

1. Using black ink, stamp image onto Image Panel piece. Color using markers and cut out.

2. Using brown ink, stamp sentiment onto Sentiment Panel piece; hand-trim a circle around sentiment.

3. Attach sentiment and image to card front using foam tape. ❮

Sources: Scor-Pal and Scor-Tape from Scor-Pal Products; cardstock and ribbon from Stampin' Up!; printed papers from Echo Park Paper Co.; stamps from Little Darlings Rubber Stamps; paper flowers from Wild Orchid Crafts; die from MAGNOLIA-licious.

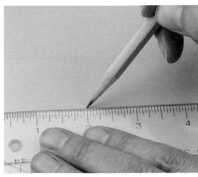

[Photo 4]

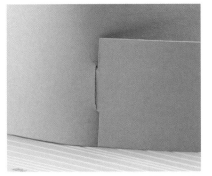

[Photo 5]

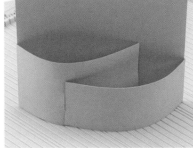

[Photo 6]

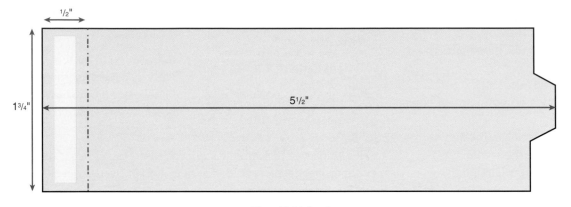

Flexy Fold Card
Top Panel Pattern

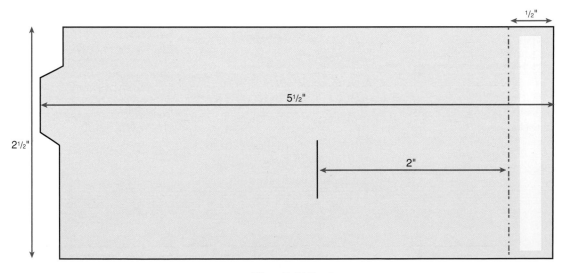

Flexy Fold Card
Bottom Panel Pattern

Template Legend
· – · · – · Score line, mountain fold
——— Cutting line
▢ Outside/right side
Scor-Tape placement
(on inside/wrong side)

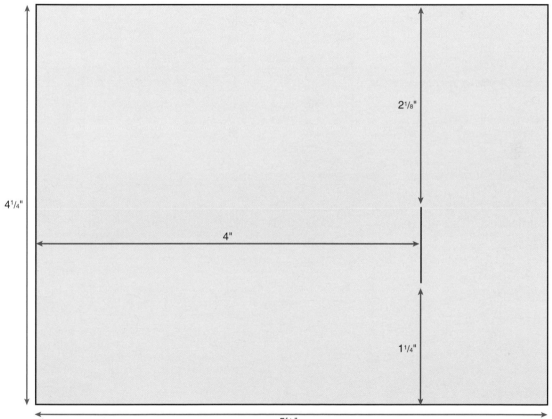

4¹/₄"

2¹/₈"

4"

1¹/₄"

5¹/₂"

Flexy Fold Card
Card Base Pattern

Materials

- › Scor-Pal
- › Scor-Tape
- › Printed papers: Country Estate collection, Garden Gala Welcome Gate
- › Cardboard
- › Country Estate Alpha Stickers
- › Brown ink pad (optional)
- › Crochet trim
- › Green rose ribbon
- › Clockface (#K1839)
- › Clock mechanism and hands
- › Punches: small hole, decorative-edge (optional)
- › Dies: Reindeer Flight (#656923), Wreath Christmas (#655537), corner flourish
- › Stapler
- › Ruler
- › Adhesive foam tape

House Clock

Design by **Virginia Nebel**

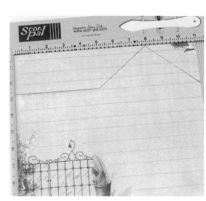

[Photo 1]

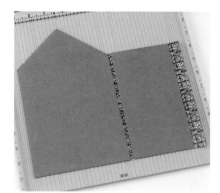

[Photo 2]

[Photo 3]

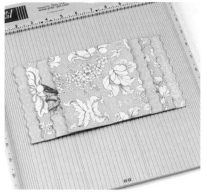

[Photo 4]   [Photo 5]   [Photo 6]

Project note: *Decorate clock with printed papers, ribbon, trim and stickers as desired.*

Pieces to Cut

Clock Body: Two 11 x 10-inch Welcome Gate paper

Clock Body Backing: Two 11 x 10-inch cardboard

Layer A: 5½ x 5½-inch Breezeway paper

Layer B: 7 x 5½-inch Restful Retreat paper

Layer C: 8½ x 5½-inch Breezeway paper

Layer D: 10 x 5½-inch Restful Retreat paper

Scoring & Assembling
Body of Clock

1. With long edge of Clock Body piece at top fence, score at 1-inch and 5-inch marks. Make a light pencil mark along top edge of paper at 8 inches.

2. Starting at left edge, draw a light pencil line 2½ inches down from top edge of Clock Body piece across entire piece. **Note:** *On Clock Body Template a portion of this pencil line is shown as the cut line extending from left side of template to 5-inch score line.*

3. Referring to Clock Body Template throughout, create roof cut lines by using ruler to draw a diagonal line from 8-inch pencil mark to where pencil mark from step 2 intersects with 5-inch score line. Draw other line in the same manner, from 8-inch pencil mark to right edge of paper (Photo 1).

4. Refer to Clock Body Template for cutting and hole punching instructions and Scor-Tape placement.

5. Repeat steps 1–4 with second Clock Body piece; do not punch a hole through this piece.

6. Trace clock body shape onto both Clock Body Backing pieces; cut out. **Note:** *The 1-inch flap of each Clock Body piece does not get a cardboard backing.* Adhere to back of each Clock Body piece as shown, leaving a small space where house will be folded (Photo 2).

7. Adhere Clock Body pieces together as shown. Attach and assemble clock to clock body as shown, layering desired printed papers and die cuts behind clockface (Photo 3).

Roof of Clock

Project note: *Punch short edges of roof pieces with a decorative-edge punch and ink brown if desired.*

1. With one edge of Layer A piece at top fence, score at 2¾-inch mark.

2. Score remaining pieces with long edge at top fence; score Layer B piece at 3½-inch mark, Layer C piece at 4¼-inch mark and Layer D at 5-inch mark.

3. Stack layer pieces on top of each other aligning scored line. Staple together along score line (Photo 4). **Note:** *If desired, adhere photos and embellishments to inside layers of roof pieces, creating a cascading photo album (Photos 5–6).* ◄

Sources: *Scor-Pal and Scor-Tape from Scor-Pal Products; printed papers, Alpha Stickers, crochet trim and rose ribbon from Webster's Pages; clockface from Maya Road; dies from Sizzix.*

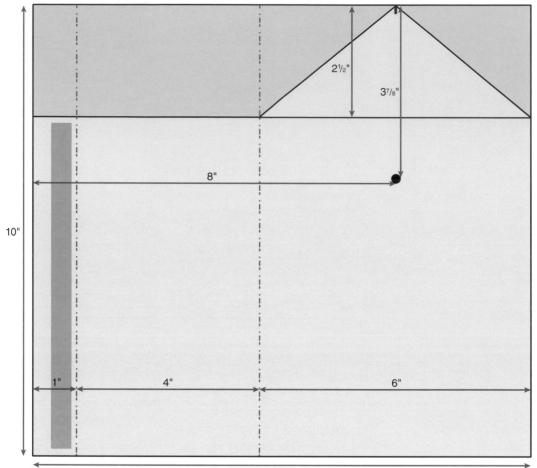

House Clock
Clock Body Template

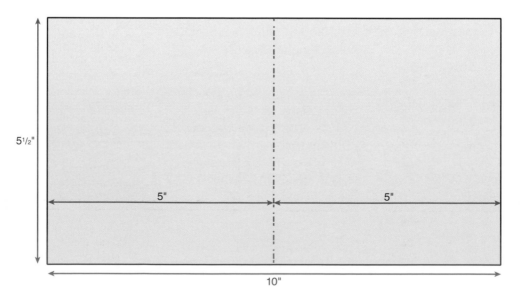

House Clock
Roof Layer D

Template Legend

- -·-·- Score line, mountain fold
- —— Cutting line
- ▌ or ▬ Mark here
- —— Pencil line
- ● Punch hole
- ▢ Outside/right side
- ▨ Cut and remove
- ▨ Scor-Tape placement (on outside/right side)

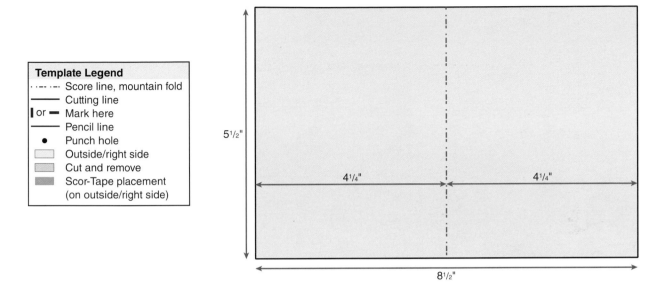

House Clock
Roof Layer C

8½"

5½"

4¼"   4¼"

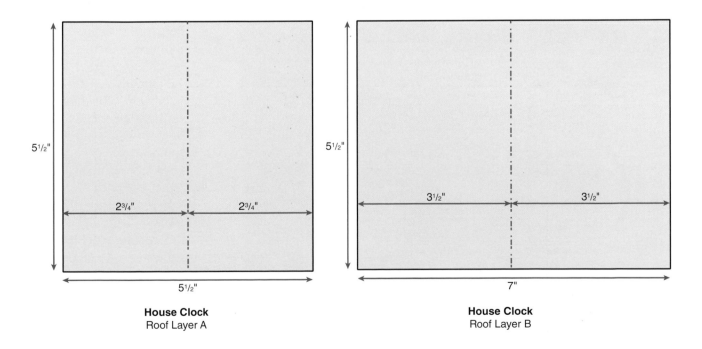

House Clock
Roof Layer A

5½"

5½"

2¾"   2¾"

House Clock
Roof Layer B

7"

5½"

3½"   3½"

Concertina Card

Design by **Gini Cagle**

Materials
› Scor-Pal
› Scor-Tape
› Printed papers:
  Forever Fall Forever Fall,
  Forever Fall Foliage
› Cardstock: black, white
  smooth, Double Dot
  Turquoise Dot
› Forever Fall stickers
› Forever Fall Noteworthy
  die cuts
› Forever Fall stamp set
› Brown dye ink pad
› Forever Fall brads
› Ribbon: 25 inches
  ⅜-inch-wide gold satin,
  12½ inches ⅝-inch-wide
  light turquoise sheer
  ruffled, 12½ inches
  ⅝-inch-wide gold sheer
  ruffled
› Love Story punch
  (#BHS623)
› Fanciful Flourish die
  (#B117)
› Die-cutting machine
› Adhesive foam squares

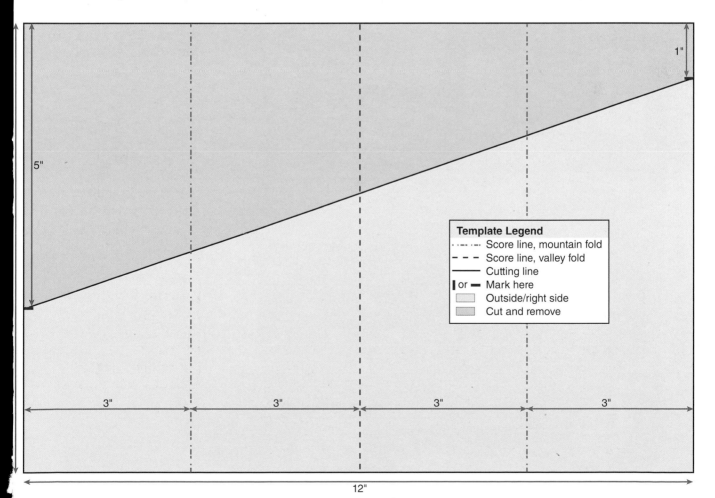

Project note:
Embellish card with printed papers, ribbon, die cuts and stamps as desired.

Piece to Cut
Card Base: 12 x 8-inch Turquoise Dot paper

Scoring & Assembling
1. With long edge of Card Base at top fence right side down, score mountain folds at 3-inch and 9-inch marks. Flip piece over and score valley fold at 6-inch mark.

2. Referring to Concertina Card Template, with long edge of piece at top fence, make a light pencil mark on left side of piece at 5-inch mark.

In the same manner, make a light pencil mark on right side of piece at 1-inch mark.

3. Using a ruler, connect pencil marks with a long diagonal pencil mark. Cut along diagonal line. Punch diagonal edge with Love Story punch as shown.

4. Refer to Concertina Card Template for folding instructions. Decorate as desired. ❮

Sources: *Scor-Pal and Scor-Tape from Scor-Pal Products; printed papers, stickers, die cuts, stamp set and brad from Bo-Bunny Press; ink pad from Clearsnap Inc.; ribbon from May Arts; punch from Blue Hills Studio; die from Cheery Lynn Designs; foam squares from Helmar.*

5"

1"

3" | 3" | 3" | 3"

12"

Template Legend
- ·–·–· Score line, mountain fold
- – – – Score line, valley fold
- —— Cutting line
- ▐ or ▬ Mark here
- ▢ Outside/right side
- ▢ Cut and remove

Concertina Card
Concertina Card Template

Materials
› Scor-Pal
› Scor-Tape
› Graphic 45 Le Cirque collection printed papers
› Black brad
› Punches: Iron Gate edge, 2-inch circle, ⅝-inch circle, 1-inch circle, 1¼-inch circle
› Large Labels die templates (#S4-168)
› Die-cutting machine
› Craft knife
› Hot-glue gun

Circus Engine

Design by **Katie Tate**

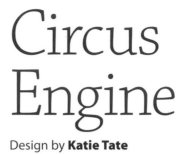

Add quilt batting to the chimney for smoke. **Tip**

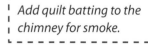

[Photo 1]

[Photo 2]

[Photo 3]

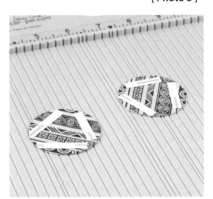

[Photo 4]

[Photo 5]

Pieces to Cut

Engine Cabin: 7¼ x 6-inch Magnifique paper

Window Frames: Four 2 x 2-inch Le Cirque paper

Engine Cover: 6½ x 3½-inch Le Cirque paper

Front/back of Engine Cover: Two 2-inch circles Magnifique paper

Top Border Engine Cabin: 8½ x ⅝-inch strip Le Cirque paper

Bottom Border Engine: 13 x 1¼-inch strip Le Cirque paper

Wheels: Four 10 x ¾-inch strips Le Cirque paper

Wheel Center: Eight ⅝-inch circles Bohemian paper

Flagpole: ¾ x 4-inch Bohemian Floral paper

Flag: 2⅝ x 1-inch Borders paper

Chimney: 3 x 2½-inch Magnifique paper

Chimney Collar: 1¼-inch circle Magnifique paper

Scoring & Assembling

Engine Cabin
1. With long edge of Engine Cabin piece at top fence, score at ¼-inch, 1¾-inch, 3¾-inch and 5¼-inch marks.

2. Rotate right, with short edge at top fence, score at 1-inch and 5-inch marks.

3. Referring to photo and Engine Cabin Template and using 1¾ x 1⅜-inch Large Labels die, die-cut label windows at the top of each side of Engine Cabin piece.

4. Using 1¾ x 1⅜-inch and 1⅛ x ⅞-inch Large Label dies, die-cut four frames from Window Frames pieces. Adhere over windows.

5. Refer to Engine Cabin Template for cutting instructions and Scor-Tape placement.

6. Fold Engine Cabin around on itself, making a box. Secure tabs with Scor-Tape (Photos 1–3).

7. Punch one edge of Top Border Engine Cabin piece with Iron Gate edge punch. Wrap and adhere around top of Engine Cabin.

Engine Cover
1. With long edge of Engine Cover piece at top fence, score at ¼-inch intervals across whole length of piece. Rotate right, with short edge at top fence, score at ½-inch and 3-inch marks. Referring to Engine Cover Template for cutting instructions, use craft knife to cut ¾-inch circle for Chimney and small hole for Flagpole. ***Tip:*** *If unsure about hole sizes, try making flag pole and chimney first. Then uses these pieces to trace hole size onto wrong side of Engine Cover piece.*

2. Place Scor-Tape all around edges of each of the Front/Back of Engine Cover pieces. Add Scor-Tape to first two scored sections as shown (Photo 4).

3. Attach two ends of Engine Cover piece together to form a tube, using scored lines to help create a neat circle (Photo 5).

4. Fold flaps on one end of Engine Cover piece under neatly and attach a Front/Back of Engine Cover piece over this end.

5. Repeat step 4 with remaining end of Engine Cover piece.

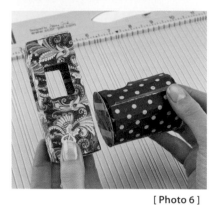

[Photo 6]

[Photo 7]

[Photo 8]

6. Attach Engine Cover to cabin using Scor-Tape (Photo 6).

7. Punch both long edges of Bottom Border Engine piece using Iron Gate edge punch.

8. Wrap punched borders around base of engine and roof of cabin.

Wheels
1. Referring to Rosettes technique, create four rosettes from Wheels pieces.

2. Using hot glue, adhere a Wheel Center to front and back of each rosette Wheel.

3. Attach Wheels to engine as shown using hot glue.

Flagpole
1. With short edge of Flagpole piece at top fence, score at ⅛-inch intervals along length and roll to form Flagpole.

2. Attach ends with Scor-Tape. Attach Flag piece to Flagpole and glue brad into top.

3. Insert Flag through Flagpole hole in Engine Cover.

Chimney
1. With long edge of Chimney piece at top fence, score at ¼-inch intervals. Roll to form a tube. Attach ends using Scor-Tape.

2. Punch a 1-inch circle through center of Chimney Collar piece.

3. Insert Chimney through Chimney hole in Engine Cover (Photo 7).

4. Slip collar over Chimney and glue in place. This will cover join of Chimney and engine (Photo 8). ❰

Sources: *Scor-Pal and Scor-Tape from Scor-Pal Products; printed papers from Graphic 45; edge punch from Martha Stewart Crafts; die templates and die-cutting machine from Spellbinders™ Paper Arts.*

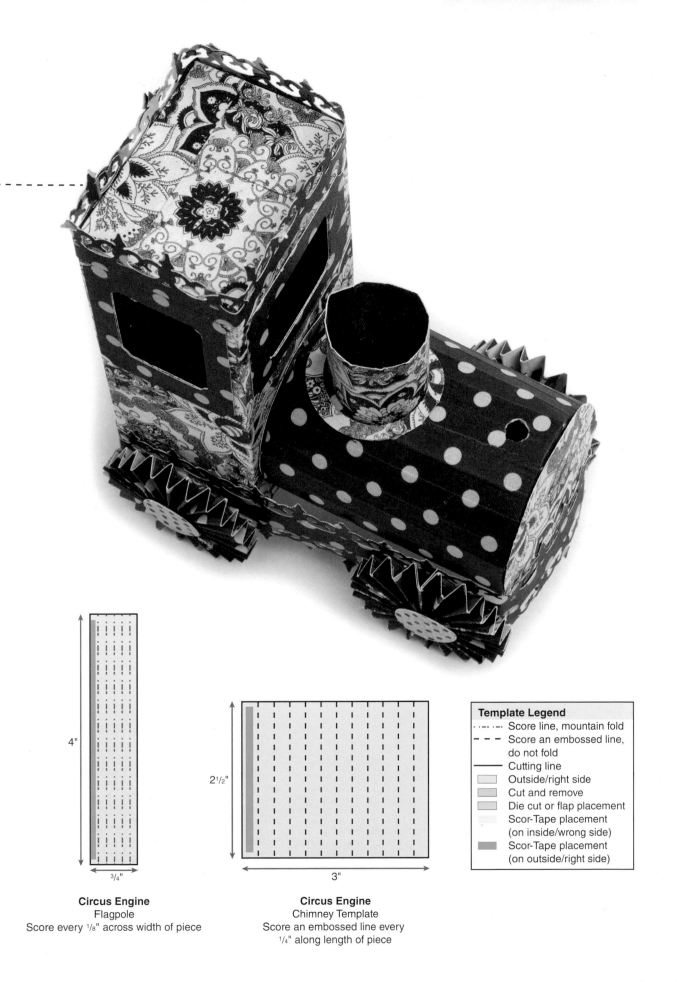

Template Legend
- ·—·—· Score line, mountain fold
- – – – Score an embossed line, do not fold
- —— Cutting line
- ▢ Outside/right side
- ▨ Cut and remove
- ▨ Die cut or flap placement
- ▢ Scor-Tape placement (on inside/wrong side)
- ▨ Scor-Tape placement (on outside/right side)

4"

³/₄"

Circus Engine
Flagpole
Score every ¹/₈" across width of piece

2¹/₂"

3"

Circus Engine
Chimney Template
Score an embossed line every
¹/₄" along length of piece

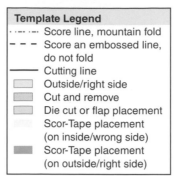

Template Legend
- · — · · — Score line, mountain fold
- – – – Score an embossed line, do not fold
- —— Cutting line
- Outside/right side
- Cut and remove
- Die cut or flap placement
- Scor-Tape placement (on inside/wrong side)
- Scor-Tape placement (on outside/right side)

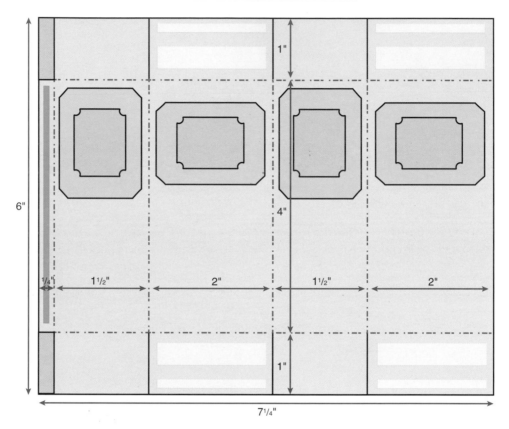

6"

4"

1"

¼" 1½" 2" 1½" 2"

1"

7¼"

Circus Engine
Engine Cabin Template

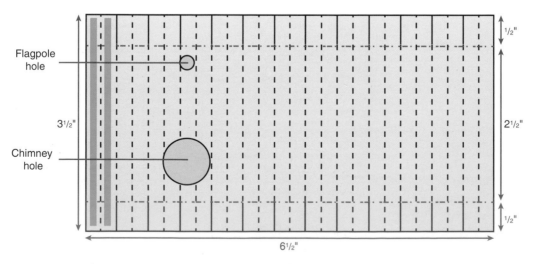

Flagpole hole

Chimney hole

3½"

½"

2½"

½"

6½"

Circus Engine
Engine Cover Template
Score an embossed line every ¼" along length of piece

Circus Train Cars

Project note: *Refer to Box Basics section when assembling train cars.*

Elephant Circus Car
Design by **Gini Cagle**

Pieces to Cut
Car: 11 x 12-inch black cardstock

Window Panel: 3¾ x 3¾-inch transparency sheet

Window Frame: 3¾ x 3¾-inch printed paper

Car Top: 6½ x 4½-inch black cardstock

Sides of Car Top: Two 7¼ x 1¾-inch black cardstock

Wheels: Four ¾ x 10-inch printed paper

Wheel Backs: Four 1-inch circles black cardstock

Scoring & Assembling
Circus Car
1. With short edge of Car piece at top fence, score at 4-inch and 7-inch marks.

2. With long edge of Car piece at top fence, score at 4-inch and 8-inch marks.

3. Refer to Car Template for cutting instructions and Scor-Tape placement. **Note:** *Using a pencil, lightly draw cutting lines onto piece before cutting.*

4. Referring to Car Template for placement, die-cut a 3 x 3⅜-inch Labels Twenty-Two label from front of Car piece. Repeat die-cutting process, die-cutting a window from Window Frame piece.

5. Assemble car. Adhere Window Panel and Window Frame in place.

6. Stamp elephant onto white smooth cardstock; color using markers.

7. Cut out elephant image, leaving a 1½-inch flap below feet. Fold flap making a stand and adhere inside Circus Car as shown.

Car Top
Project note: *When constructing Car Top Sides, refer to Sides of Car Top Template when making*

pencil marks. Extend marks across cardstock piece, creating guidelines to draw cutting lines.

1. With long edge of Car Top piece at top fence, score at 1-inch, 3¼-inch and 5½-inch marks.

2. With short edge of Car Top piece at top fence, score at ¾-inch and 3¾-inch marks.

3. Refer to Car Top Template for cutting instructions and Scor-Tape placement. Fold down flaps at score lines and peak of piece.

4. Set aside.

5. Referring to Sides of Car Top Template and on wrong side of one Sides of Car Top piece, make pencil marks along long edge at 1⁹⁄₁₆ inches, 3⅝ inches and 5¹¹⁄₁₆ inches.

6. In the same manner, make pencil marks on both short edges of piece 1 inch from bottom edge.

7. Repeat steps 5 and 6 with second Sides of Car Top piece. Referring to Sides of Car Top Template, draw cutting lines and cut out both pieces. Referring to

Materials
› Scor-Pal
› Scor-Tape
› Cardstock: black, white smooth
› Blissful Felicity double-sided printed paper
› Transparency sheet
› Elephant stamp
› Black dye ink pad
› Markers
› 15½ inches 1-inch-wide gray flower ribbon
› 4 decorative yellow buttons
› Clear star stickpin
› Labels Twenty-Two die templates (#S4-346)
› Die-cutting machine
› Ruler
› Adhesive foam squares
› Hot-glue gun

Sides of Car Top Template, draw cutting lines and cut out both pieces (Photo 1).

8. On each piece, line up the 1⁹⁄₁₆-inch mark with any groove on Scor-Pal and score. Repeat for 5¹¹⁄₁₆-inch mark. Referring to Sides of Car Top Template as needed.

9. Refer to Sides of Car Top Template for Scor-Tape placement. *Note: Do not remove back liner of Scor-Tape until ready to adhere pieces together.*

10. Adhere center of one Sides of Car Top piece to front flaps of Car Top piece, aligning peaks (Photos 2–3).

11. Adhere side flaps of Sides of Car Top piece to side flaps of Car Top piece.

12. Repeat steps 10 and 11 for second Sides of Car Top piece and remaining side of Car Top.

Wheels
1. Referring to Rosettes technique, create four rosettes from Wheels pieces.

2. Using hot glue, adhere a Wheel Back to back of each rosette wheel. Embellish center fronts of wheels with buttons.

3. Attach wheels to car as shown using hot glue.

Flag
1. Cut a 2¾ x ⅝-inch piece from printed paper and a 3 x ⅜-inch piece from black cardstock. Cut a V-notch at one short edge of both pieces.

Embellish assembled car and car top as desired using printed paper and ribbon. Tip

2. Adhere pieces together as shown, sandwiching stickpin between them. Curve pieces with fingers as desired.

3. Insert stickpin through top of Car Top. Stack three foam squares together and stick end of stickpin through squares. Push foam squares to inside top of Car Top; adhere stickpin in place.

Sources: *Scor-Pal and Scor-Tape from Scor-Pal Products; cardstock from Bazzill Basics Paper Inc.; printed paper from Authentique; stamp from MAGNOLIA-licious; flower ribbon from Webster's Pages; die templates and die-cutting machine from Spellbinders™ Paper Arts.*

[Photo 1]

[Photo 2]

[Photo 3]

Lion Circus Car
Design by **Lisa Andrews**

Pieces to Cut

Car Base: 7 x 8-inch Flying High paper

Car Top: 5⅛ x 6⅛-inch Magnifique paper

Inside Platform: 4⅞ x 5⅞-inch Flying High paper

Corner Posts: Four ¾ x 4¾-inch black cardstock

Wheels: Four ¾ x 10-inch black cardstock

Wheel Backs: Eight 1½-inch circles black cardstock

Banner: Four 3½ x 1½-inch Magnifique paper

Scoring & Assembling
Car Base

1. With short edge of Car Base piece at top fence, score at 1-inch, 2-inch, 5-inch and 6-inch marks.

Materials
› Scor-Pal
› Scor-Tape
› Cardstock: black, white smooth
› Le Cirque printed papers: Flying High, Magnifique, Le Cirque Tags
› Lion stamp
› Black dye ink pad
› Markers
› Bamboo skewers
› 4 silver beads
› 4 black flower brads
› Punches: ⅛-inch hole, 1½-inch circle
› Glue
› Hot-glue gun

2. With long edge of Car Base piece at top fence, score at 1-inch, 2-inch, 6-inch and 7-inch marks.

3. Refer to Car Base Template for cutting instructions and Scor-Tape placement, leaving tape backing in place until adhering pieces together.

4. Fold at score lines; use scoring tool to burnish folds.

5. Assemble Car Base.

Inside Platform

1. Score Inside Platform piece at 1 inch on all sides.

2. Refer to Inside Platform Template for cutting instructions, Scor-Tape placement and hole-punching instructions; holes are

½ inch apart. **Note:** *Mark where holes will be punched with a pencil before punching.* These holes are where bamboo skewers will go to create the cage.

3. Fold at score lines. Assemble platform.

4. Adhere inside Car Base using Scor-Tape as needed.

5. Cut 16 skewers approximately 4 inches long (cage bars) and four skewers approximately 3½ inches long (flagpoles). Color bamboo skewers black.

6. Score each of the Corner Post pieces at ⅜ inch along their length. Fold in half. Referring to Inside Platform Template, adhere bottom of Corner Posts to corners

of platform. Adhere a strip of Scor-Tape along top edges of Corner Post pieces.

7. Stamp lion twice onto white smooth cardstock; color using markers and cut out.

8. Adhere tops of lions together, prop bottom of lions as needed with cardstock and adhere inside Car Base.

Car Top

1. Score Car Top piece at 1 inch on all sides.

2. Refer to Car Top Template for cutting instructions, Scor-Tape placement and hole-punching instructions.

3. Fold at score lines. Assemble Car Top.

4. Referring to photo, fold Banner pieces in half and hand-cut into flag shapes. Wrap a banner piece around top section of flagpoles, adhering as needed. Attach a bead on top of each flagpole using glue.

Wheels

1. Referring to Rosettes technique, create four rosettes from Wheels pieces.

2. Using hot glue, adhere Wheel Backs to back of each rosette Wheel. Embellish center fronts of Wheels with brads.

3. Attach Wheels to car as shown using hot glue.

Car Assembly

1. Insert all cage bars in holes on the Inside Platform.

2. Apply a length of Scor-Tape to inside edges of Car Top. Put top in place, adhering tops of cage bars and Corner Posts to Scor-Tape.

3. Insert flagpoles into holes on Car Top. Press ends of flagpoles into Scor-Tape on top edges of Corner Posts to secure in place.

Sources: *Scor-Pal and Scor-Tape from Scor-Pal Products; cardstock from Bazzill Basics Paper Inc.; printed papers from Graphic 45; stamp from MAGNOLIA-licious; beads and brads from Michaels Stores Inc.; Crop-A-Dile hole punch from We R Memory Keepers.*

Monkey Circus Car
Design by **Lisa Andrews**

Materials
› Scor-Pal
› Scor-Tape
› Cardstock: white smooth, black
› Le Cirque printed papers: Under the Big Top, Magnifique, Le Cirque Borders, Le Cirque Tags
› Monkey stamp
› Black dye ink pad
› Markers
› Small branch
› Brown/white baker's twine
› 6 white flat-backed pearl gems
› Deckled Rectangles LG die templates (#S4-202)
› Die-cutting machine
› Craft knife
› Hot-glue gun

Pieces to Cut

Car Base: 11 x 12-inch Magnifique paper

Car Top: 5⅛ x 6⅛-inch Under the Big Top paper

Wheels: Four ¾ x 10-inch Under the Big Top paper

Wheels Backs: Four 1½-inch circles black cardstock

Scoring & Assembling

Car Base
1. With short edge of Car Base piece at top fence, score at 4-inch and 7-inch marks.

2. With long edge of Car Base piece at top fence, score at 4-inch and 8-inch marks.

3. Refer to Car Base Template for cutting instructions and Scor-Tape placement. **Note:** *Using a pencil, lightly draw cutting lines onto piece before cutting.*

4. Referring to Car Base Template for placement, die-cut a 2⅜ x 3⅛-inch Deckled Rectangle from front of Car Base piece.

5. Assemble car.

6. Stamp monkey onto white smooth cardstock; color using markers and cut out.

Car Top
1. Score Car Top piece at 1 inch on all sides.

2. Refer to Car Top Template for cutting instructions and Scor-Tape placement.

3. Fold at score lines. Assemble Car Top.

Wheels
1. Referring to Rosettes technique, create four rosettes from Wheels pieces.

2. Using hot glue, adhere Wheel Backs to back of each rosette Wheel. Embellish center fronts of Wheels with pearl gems.

3. Attach Wheels to car as shown using hot glue.

Car Assembly
1. Cut a length of baker's twine; adhere monkey's hand to center of twine.

2. Stretch baker's twine across top of Car Base, positioning monkey as desired. Adhere ends of baker's twine to sides of Car Base and trim as needed. Place small branch inside car; hot glue in place if desired.

3. Adhere Car Top to top of Car Base. ❮

***Sources:** Scor-Pal and Scor-Tape from Scor-Pal Products; cardstock from Bazzill Basics Paper Inc.; printed papers from Graphic 45; stamp from MAGNOLIA-licious; die templates and die-cutting machine from Spellbinders™ Paper Arts.*

Embellish assembled car and Car Top as desired using printed papers and remaining pearl gems. Tip

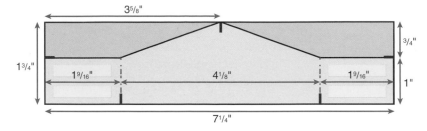

Circus Train Cars
Elephant Circus Car
Sides of Car Top Template

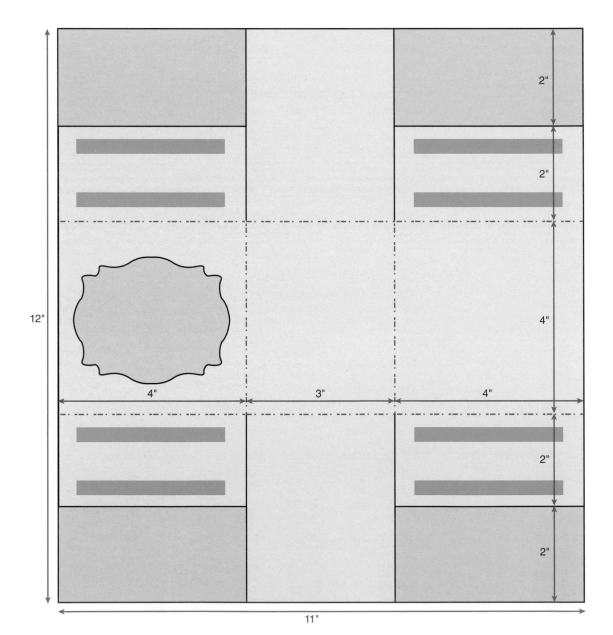

Circus Train Cars
Elephant Circus Car
Car Template

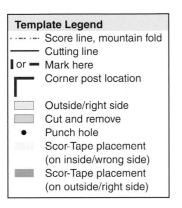

Template Legend
- ·–·–·– Score line, mountain fold
- —— Cutting line
- ▌ or ▬ Mark here
- └ Corner post location
- ▢ Outside/right side
- ▨ Cut and remove
- • Punch hole
- ▨ Scor-Tape placement (on inside/wrong side)
- ▨ Scor-Tape placement (on outside/right side)

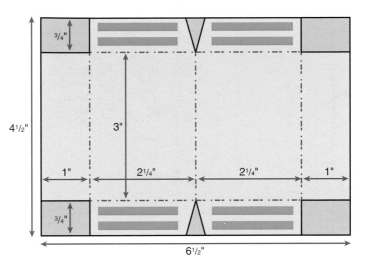

Circus Train Cars
Elephant Circus Car
Car Top Template

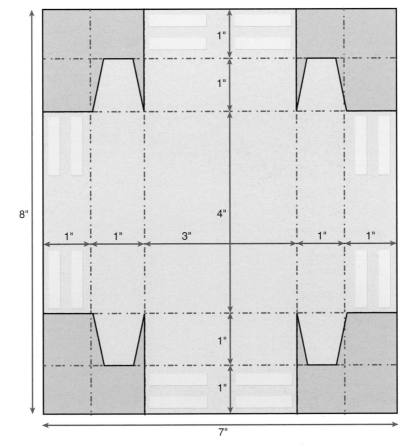

Circus Train Cars
Lion Circus Car
Car Base Template

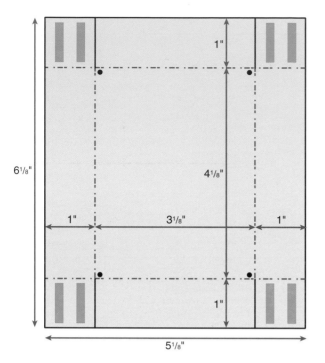

Circus Train Cars
Lion Circus Car
Car Top Template

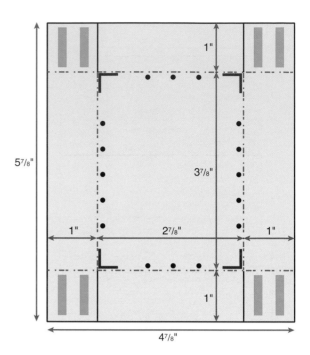

Circus Train Cars
Lion Circus Car
Inside Platform Template

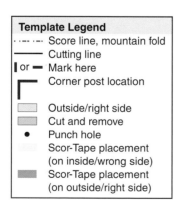

Template Legend

- · — · · — · Score line, mountain fold
- ———— Cutting line
- ▐ or ▬ Mark here
- ⌐ Corner post location

- ▢ Outside/right side
- ▩ Cut and remove
- ● Punch hole
- ▢ Scor-Tape placement
  (on inside/wrong side)
- ▤ Scor-Tape placement
  (on outside/right side)

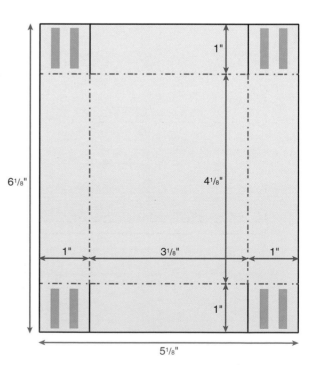

Circus Train Cars
Monkey Circus Car
Car Top Template

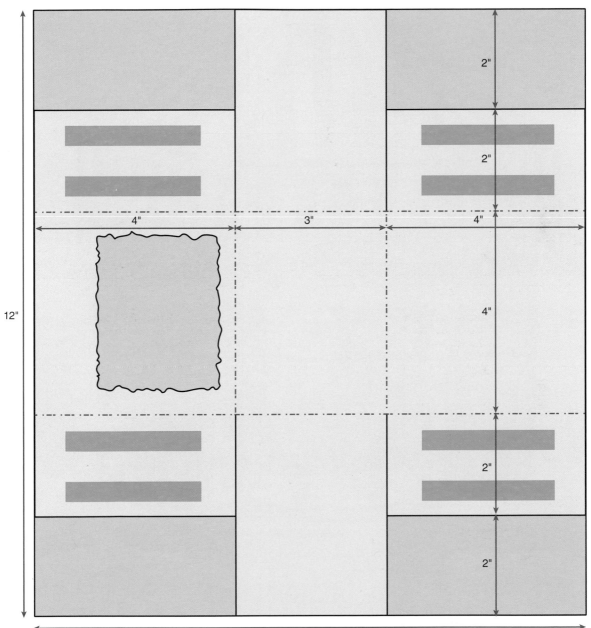

Circus Train Cars
Monkey Circus Car
Car Base Template

Circus Tent

Design by **Gini Cagle**

Materials

› Scor-Pal
› Scor-Tape
› Cardstock: blue pearlescent, red, yellow, clear
› Le Cirque 12 x 12 Paper Pad
› Brown distress ink pad
› Red color sprinkles
› Red/white baker's twine
› Small white self-adhesive pearls
› Toothpick

› Red thread
› Sewing machine
› Die templates: Labels Four (#S4-190), Banner Basics One (#S5-044)
› Die-cutting machine
› Paper piercer
› Adhesive foam tape
› Hot-glue gun
› Clear-drying glue

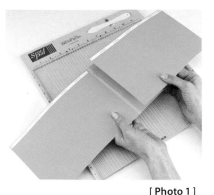

[Photo 1]

[Photo 2]

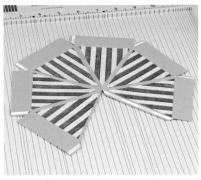

[Photo 3]

Project note: *Decorate tent with desired die-cut pieces of cardstock and printed papers, distress ink, color sprinkles, baker's twine and self-adhesive pearls.*

Pieces to Cut

Wall: Two 6 x 12-inch blue pearlescent cardstock

Window: Three 3 x 5-inch clear cardstock

Roof: Two 8½ x 11-inch blue pearlescent cardstock

Roof Pendants: Six 4 x 4-inch Circus Parade paper

Floor: 8½ x 11-inch blue pearlescent cardstock

Outside Panels: Six pieces 2¾ x 4¾-inch Circus Parade paper

Inside Panels: Three 3 x 4¾-inch assorted printed papers

Scoring & Assembling

Tent Walls & Floor

1. With short edge of one Wall piece at top fence, score at 1-inch mark.

2. With long edge of same Wall piece at top fence, score at 3-inch, 6-inch and 9-inch marks.

3. Repeat steps 1 and 2 for second Wall piece.

4. Refer to Wall Pieces 1 and 2 templates for cutting and Scor-Tape placement; do not die-cut windows.

5. Adhere Wall pieces together as shown (Photo 1).

6. Adhere Outside Panels to right side of Wall pieces. **Note:** *Machine-stitch around edges of pieces before adhering if desired.*

7. Referring to Wall Pieces 1 and 2 templates for die template placement, die-cut 1¾ x 3⅛-inch Labels Four windows from Wall pieces. **Note:** *Do not choose section where Walls pieces are adhered together for die-cutting.*

8. Adhere Window pieces to inside of die-cut panels.

9. Fold 1-inch flap at top edge of Wall pieces down and adhere to inside edge. Adhere Inside Panels inside Wall pieces, cover panels that do not have windows. Adhere ½-inch flap to inside edge of opposite wall piece.

10. Using Floor Pattern, cut a tent floor from Floor piece. Refer to pattern for scoring instructions and Scor-Tape placement.

11. Referring to photo, adhere Floor to Wall pieces (Photo 2).

Tent Roof

1. Using Roof Pattern, cut two tent roof pieces from Roof pieces. Refer to pattern for scoring instructions and Scor-Tape placement.

[Photo 4]

2. Referring to photos, adhere Roof pieces together (Photos 3–4).

3. Using Roof Pendants Pattern, cut a pendant from each Roof Pendants piece. Adhere to roof as shown.

4. Cut banners from cardstock and printed paper. Adhere banner pieces together using foam tape, sandwiching toothpick between pieces. Pierce a hole through top of tent and insert toothpick, securing inside with hot glue. ❮

Sources: *Scor-Pal and Scor-Tape from Scor-Pal Products; clear cardstock from Heartfelt Creations; remaining cardstock from Bazzill Basics Paper Inc.; paper pad from Graphic 45; ink pad from Ranger Industries Inc.; color sprinkles and Flower Soft glue from Flower Soft® Inc.; baker's twine from The Twinery; self-adhesive pearls from Kaisercraft; die templates and die-cutting machine from Spellbinders™ Paper Arts.*

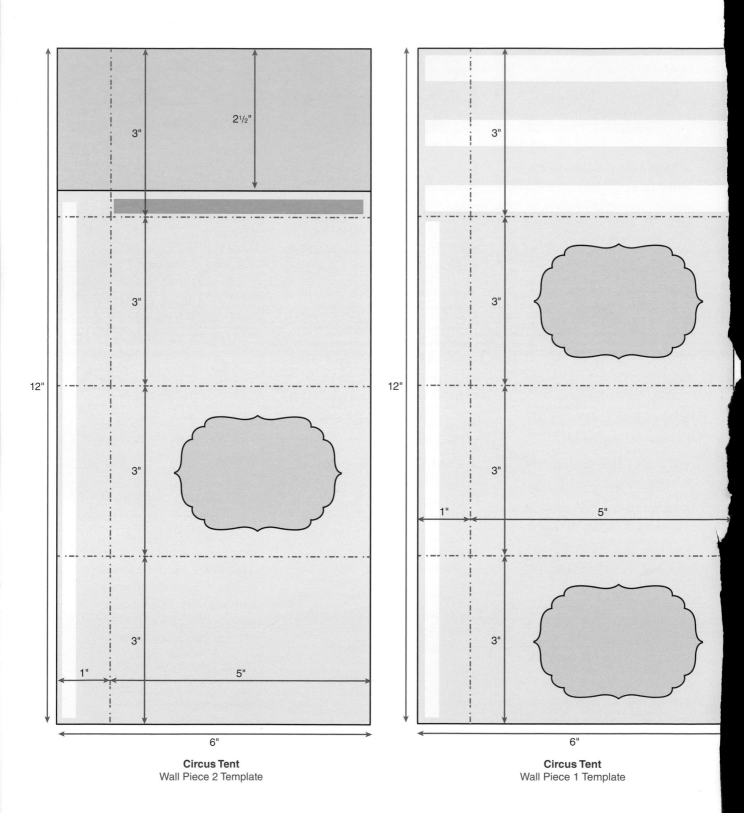

Circus Tent
Wall Piece 2 Template

Circus Tent
Wall Piece 1 Template

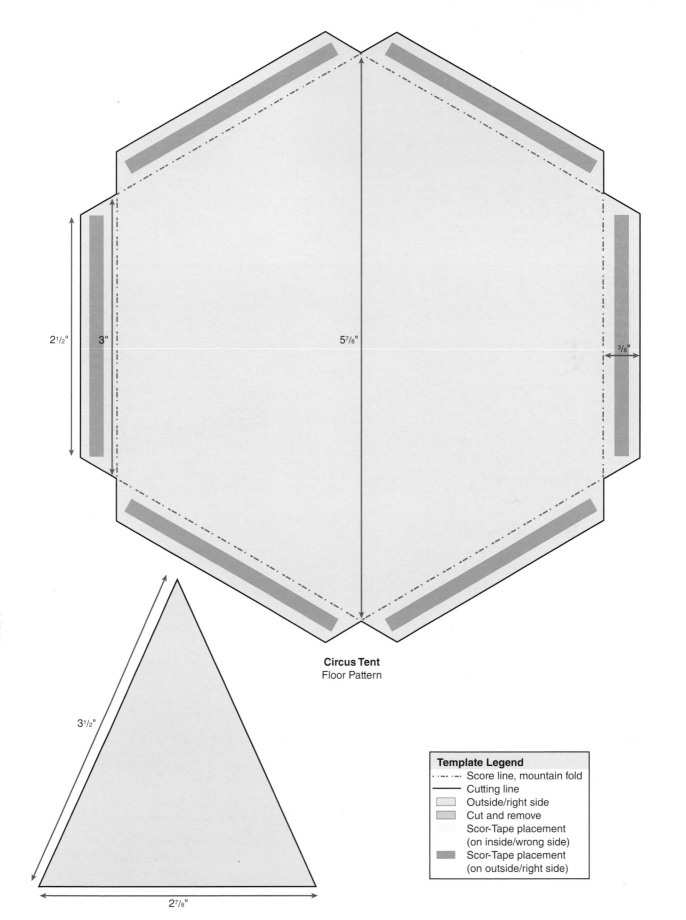

Circus Tent
Floor Pattern

2 1/2" 3" 5 7/8" 3/8"

3 1/2"

2 7/8"

Circus Tent
Roof Pendants Pattern

Template Legend

-·-·- Score line, mountain fold
——— Cutting line
Outside/right side
Cut and remove
Scor-Tape placement
(on inside/wrong side)
Scor-Tape placement
(on outside/right side)

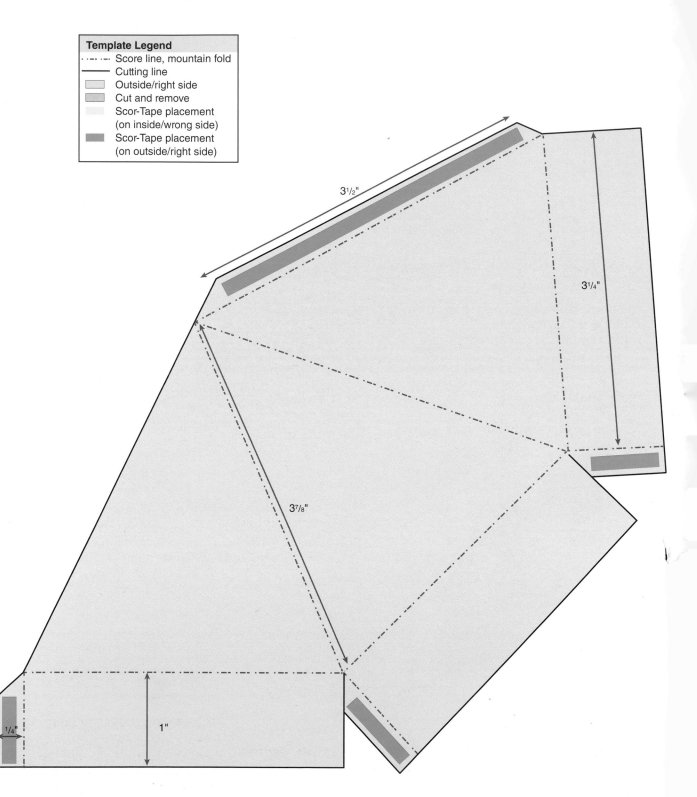

Template Legend

- ·—·—·— Score line, mountain fold
- —— Cutting line
- Outside/right side
- Cut and remove
- Scor-Tape placement (on inside/wrong side)
- Scor-Tape placement (on outside/right side)

3¹/₂"

3¹/₄"

3⁷/₈"

1"

¹/₄"

Circus Tent
Roof Pattern

Circus Popcorn Stand

Design by **Diane Zechman**

Materials
› Scor-Pal
› Scor-Tape
› Cardstock: rust, black, white smooth
› Le Cirque printed papers: Greatest Show on Earth, Circus Parade, Wizards of Wonders
› Stamps: Circus Tilda, Popcorn, Mini Popcorn
› Black dye ink pad
› Black permanent markers
› Copic® markers
› 2 craft sticks
› 2 toothpicks
› 2 bamboo skewers
› Scallop Edge Border punch
› Small Scalloped Octagons die templates (#S4-188)
› Die-cutting machine
› Adhesive foam tape

Project note: Refer to Box Basics section when assembling base and roof. Use printed papers, toothpicks and die-cut pieces to decorate stand as desired.

Pieces to Cut
Base: 6 x 8-inch rust cardstock

Roof: 3 x 5-inch rust cardstock

Awning: 2 x 4-inch Circus Parade paper

Back Wall: 3⅞ x 4½-inch Circus Parade paper

Back Supports: Two 1 x 4½-inch Greatest Show on Earth paper

Scoring & Assembling
Stand Base
1. With short edge of Base piece at top fence, score at 2-inch and 4-inch marks.

2. With long edge of Base piece at top fence, score at 2-inch and 6-inch marks.

3. Refer to Base Template for cutting instructions and Scor-Tape placement.

4. Assemble base.

Stand Roof
1. Score Roof piece at ½-inch mark on all sides.

2. Refer to Roof Template for cutting instructions and Scor-Tape placement.

3. Assemble roof.

Awning & Back Supports
1. Punch one long edge of Awning piece with punch.

2. With short edge of Awning piece at top fence faceup, score a valley fold at ½-inch mark. Flip piece over and score a mountain fold at 1½-inch mark. ***Note:*** *When scoring this piece, place unpunched edge against straight left edge of Scor-Pal.*

[Photo 1]

[Photo 2]

[Photo 3]

3. Refer to Awning Template for Scor-Tape placement. Set aside.

4. Wrap around and adhere a Back Support piece to a craft stick. Repeat with remaining craft stick.

5. Cut two 4½-inch pieces from bamboo skewers; color black.

Assembling
1. Attach Back Supports and bamboo skewers inside of Stand Base as shown (Photo 1).

2. Adhere Back Wall piece to back of Base piece aligning bottom edges.

3. Adhere Awning piece to inside edge of roof (Photo 2).

4. Adhere Roof to top of bamboo skewers and Back Supports (Photo 3).

5. Stamp images onto white smooth cardstock; color with markers and cut out. Adhere to popcorn stand using foam tape as desired. ◄

Sources: Scor-Pal, Scor-Tape from Scor-Pal Products; cardstock and punch from Stampin' Up!; printed papers from Graphic 45; stamp from MAGNOLIA-licious; ink pad from Imagine Crafts/Tsukineko; markers from Imagination International Inc.; die templates from Spellbinders™ Paper Arts.

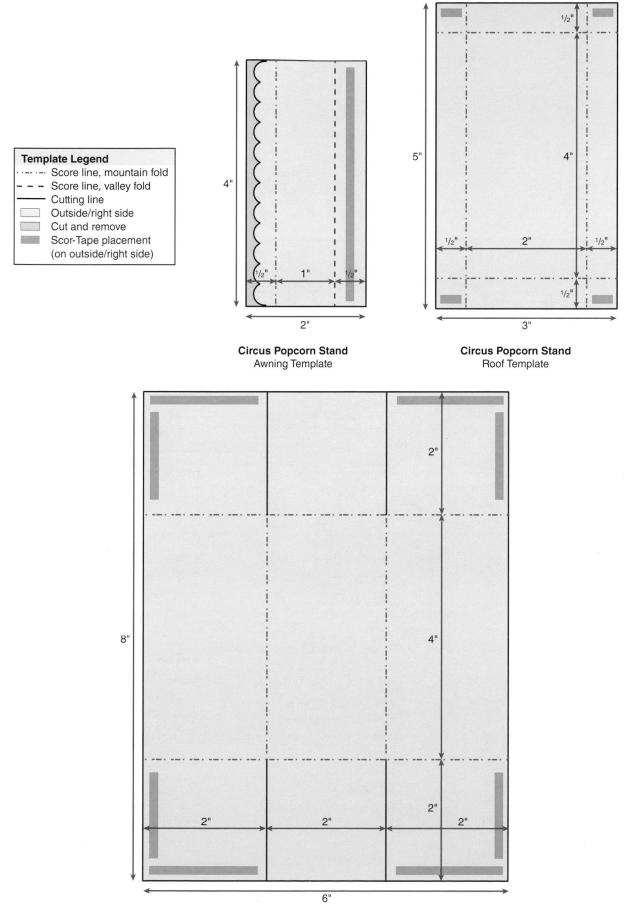

Template Legend
- ·—·—· Score line, mountain fold
- – – – Score line, valley fold
- —— Cutting line
- ☐ Outside/right side
- ☐ Cut and remove
- ▮ Scor-Tape placement (on outside/right side)

Circus Popcorn Stand
Awning Template

Circus Popcorn Stand
Roof Template

Circus Popcorn Stand
Base Template

Card & Gift Box in One

Design by **Patti Jo Skogquist**

Materials
- Scor-Pal
- Scor-Tape
- Cardstock: turquoise, white smooth, green, dark teal, light yellow
- Mini Sweet Tilda stamp
- Dye ink pads: black, blue distress, green distress
- Markers
- 22 inches ¼-inch-wide turquoise decorative ribbon
- 2 silver brads
- Square Lattice Textured embossing folder
- Die templates: Classic Ovals SM (#S4-112), Vintage Tag, Leaf & Swirl, Old Swedish Lace, Doily Flowers, Rose Leaf, Grass, Butterflies
- Die-cutting and embossing machine
- Paper piercer
- Craft sponge
- Computer with printer (optional)

Project note: *Decorate box sleeve using die-cut cardstock pieces as desired. Decorate inside of sleeve with colored die-cut stamped image, computer generated sentiment and die-cut cardstock pieces.*

Pieces to Cut

Project note: *Emboss white smooth cardstock pieces using Square Lattice Textured embossing folder to create white embossed cardstock pieces.*

Box Sleeve: 10¼ x 3½-inch turquoise cardstock

Sleeve Sides: Three 3¼ x ¾-inch white embossed cardstock

Box Sleeve Panels: Two 3¼ x 2⅛-inch white embossed cardstock

Box: 4 x 7-inch turquoise cardstock

Box Ends: Two 2 x ¾-inch white embossed cardstock

Scoring & Assembling
Box Sleeve

1. With long edge of Box Sleeve piece at top fence, score at ½-inch, 2¾-inch, 3¾-inch, 6-inch, 7-inch and 9¼-inch marks.

2. Refer to Box Sleeve template for Scor-Tape placement.

3. Adhere ½-inch flap to middle 1-inch section, creating a box sleeve (Photo 1).

4. Referring to Box Sleeve template, adhere a 16-inch length of ribbon to box sleeve; position ribbon so it will be able to tie a bow over 1-inch flap opening.

5. Adhere Box Sleeve Panels and Sleeve Sides to Box Sleeve as shown.

Box

1. With long edge of Box piece at top fence, score at ⅞-inch and 1¾-inch marks. Repeat on opposite end of piece.

2. With short edge of Box piece at top fence, score at ⅞-inch mark. Repeat on opposite end of piece.

3. Refer to Box template for cutting instructions and Scor-Tape placement.

[Photo 1]

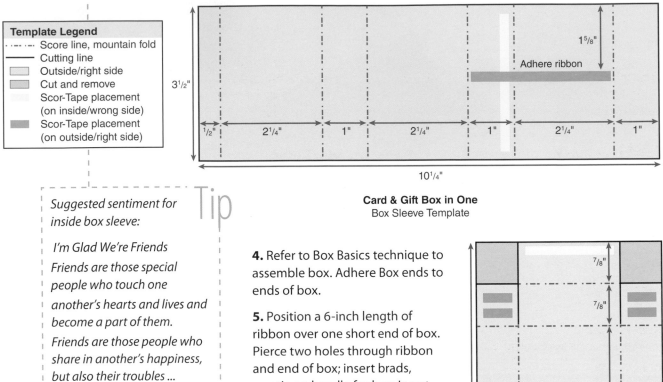

Template Legend
- ·—··—··— Score line, mountain fold
- ——— Cutting line
- Outside/right side
- Cut and remove
- Scor-Tape placement (on inside/wrong side)
- Scor-Tape placement (on outside/right side)

1⁵/₈"

Adhere ribbon

3¹/₂"

¹/₂" 2¹/₄" 1" 2¹/₄" 1" 2¹/₄" 1"

10¹/₄"

Card & Gift Box in One
Box Sleeve Template

Suggested sentiment for inside box sleeve:

I'm Glad We're Friends

Friends are those special people who touch one another's hearts and lives and become a part of them.

Friends are those people who share in another's happiness, but also their troubles ... sharing in feelings and fondest dreams.

Thank you for being such a wonderful friend.

Thank you for being you!

4. Refer to Box Basics technique to assemble box. Adhere Box ends to ends of box.

5. Position a 6-inch length of ribbon over one short end of box. Pierce two holes through ribbon and end of box; insert brads, creating a handle for box. Insert box into box sleeve. ❮

Sources: *Scor-Pal and Scor-Tape from Scor-Pal Products; stamp, Vintage Tag die, Leaf & Swirl die, Old Swedish Lace die, Doily Flowers die, Rose Leaf die, Grass die and Butterflies die from MAGNOLIA-licious; distress ink pads from Ranger Industries Inc.; embossing folder from Stampin' Up!; Classic Ovals SM die templates from Spellbinders™ Paper Arts.*

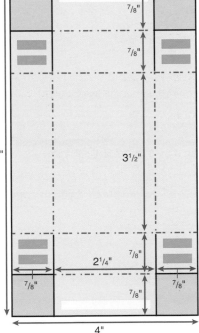

7"

7/8"

7/8"

3¹/₂"

2¹/₄" 7/8"

7/8" 7/8" 7/8"

4"

Card & Gift Box in One
Box Template

Designers

Brenda Quintana
http://qbeesquest.blogspot.ca/

Victorian Drawers, 22

Tami Mayberry
http://tamimayberry.blogspot.ca/

Basic Rosettes, 20   Cake Gift Box, 27

Julie Koerber
http://outtoimpress.blogspot.ca/

Scoring Techniques &   You Inspire Me Gatefold
   Terminology, 9   Card, 40
ABC Desk Set, 32

Kim Hughes
http://papersmooches.blogspot.ca/

Way to Go, 39

Bonnie Szwalkiewicz
http://craftiblog.wordpress.com

Rosette Christmas Trees, 42

Mindy Baxter
http://stampinmindy.blogspot.ca/

Flexy Fold Card, 44

Virginia Nebel
http://virginianebel.blogspot.ca/

House Clock, 48

Gini Cagle
http://ginicagle.blogspot.ca/

Concertina Card, 52   Circus Tent, 68
Elephant Circus Car, 59

Katie Tate
http://bothsidesofthepaper.blogspot.ca/

Circus Engine, 54

Lisa Andrews
http://scrappingwithlisa.blogspot.ca/

Lion Circus Car, 61   Monkey Circus Car, 62

Diane Zechman
http://papercookies.blogs.splitcoaststampers.com/

Circus Popcorn Stand, 73

Patti Jo Skogquist
http://pjsdesigns.blogspot.ca/

Card & Gift Box in One, 76

Contributing Designers

Diana Crick

Diana Crick is the creator of Scor-Pal and subsequent add-on products. Her visions and ideas have been re-created in many of the tutorials. Diana has always had a love for the creative world in many, many formats—her latest love being paper crafting. She also enjoys art journaling and Zentangle®, her newest passion, which she is a certified teacher of. She hopes by completing the many projects a whole new world will be discovered, with the Scor-Pal becoming one of your most valuable tools if it isn't already.

http://scor-pal.blogspot.ca/

Penny Wessenaur

Penny Wessenauer was trained in an architecture-based program of interior design, and worked for years in the field of architecture before taking an early retirement. Retirement allowed her the time to indulge in her love of paper and card making. Using her early training, she began drawing "to scale" templates for card types for others to use. The templates in this book were drawn by Penny, but have been simplified for easier reader understanding.

http://s27.photobucket.com/albums/c191/d0npen/

Buyer's Guide

Authentique
(800) 374-8070
www.authentiquepaper.com

Bazzill Basics Paper Inc.
(800) 560-1610
www.bazzillbasics.com

Blue Hills Studio
www.multishaper.com/

Bo-Bunny Press
(801) 771-4010
www.bobunny.com

Cheery Lynn Designs
(602) 385-4126
www.cheerylynndesigns.com

Clearsnap Inc.
(800) 448-4862
www.clearsnap.com

Creative Impressions Inc.
(719) 596-4860
www.creativeimpressions.com

Echo Park Paper Co.
(800) 701-1115
www.echoparkpaper.com

Fiskars
(866) 348-5661
www.fiskars.com

Flourishes
(888) 475-1575
http://flourishes.org

Flower Soft® Inc.
(877) 989-0205
www.flower-soft.com

GlueArts
(866) 889-4583
www.gluearts.com

Graphic 45
(866) 573-4806
www.g45papers.com

Heartfelt Creations
(888) 773-3088
www.heartfeltcreations.us

Helmar
www.helmarusa.com

Imagination International Inc.
(541) 684-0013
www.copicmarker.com

Imagine Crafts/Tsukineko
(425) 883-7733
www.imaginecrafts.com

Impression Obsession Inc.
(877) 259-0905
www.impression-obsession.com

Kaisercraft
(888) 684-7147
www.kaisercraft.net

Krylon
(800) 457-9566
www.krylon.com

Little Darlings Rubber Stamps
www.lovetostamp.com

MAGNOLIA-licious
(604) 594-5188
www.magnoliastamps.us

Martha Stewart Crafts
www.eksuccessbrands.com/
marthastewartcrafts

May Arts
(203) 637-8366
www.mayarts.net

Maya Road
(877) 427-7764
www.mayaroad.com

Michaels Stores Inc.
(800) 642-4235
www.michaels.com

My Favorite Things
www.mftstamps.com

Paper Smooches
(623) 533-3776
www.papersmoochesstamps.com

The Paper Studio
(480) 557-5700
www.paperstudio.com

Pink Paislee
(816) 883-8259
www.pinkpaislee.com

Prima Marketing Inc.
(909) 627-5532
www.primamarketinginc.com

Ranger Industries Inc.
(732) 389-3535
www.rangerink.com

Scor-Pal Products
(877) 629-9908
www.scor-pal.com

Sizzix
(877) 355-4766
www.sizzix.com

Spellbinders™ Paper Arts
(888) 547-0400
www.spellbinderspaperarts.com

Stampin' Up!
(800) STAMP UP (782-6787)
www.stampinup.com

Therm O Web Inc.
(800) 323-0799
www.thermowebonline.com

The Twinery
http://thetwinery.com/

Uchida of America Corp.
www.uchida.com

Want2Scrap
(260) 740-2976
www.want2scrap.com

We R Memory Keepers
(877) PICKWER (742-5937)
www.weronthenet.com

Webster's Pages
(800) 543-6104
www.websterspages.com

Wild Orchid Crafts
www.wildorchidcrafts.com

The Buyer's Guide listings are provided as a service to our readers and should not be considered an endorsement from this publication.

Score, Fold, Create!

EDITOR Tanya Fox

CREATIVE DIRECTOR Brad Snow

PUBLISHING SERVICES DIRECTOR
Brenda Gallmeyer

MANAGING EDITOR Brooke Smith

TECHNICAL EDITOR Corene Painter

GRAPHIC DESIGNER Nick Pierce

COPY SUPERVISOR Deborah Morgan

COPY EDITORS Emily Carter, Sam Schneider

PHOTOGRAPHY SUPERVISOR
Tammy Christian

PHOTO STYLISTS Tammy Liechty,
Tammy Steiner

PHOTOGRAPHY Matthew Owen

PRODUCTION ARTIST SUPERVISOR
Erin Brandt

PRODUCTION ARTIST Nicole Gage

TECHNICAL ARTIST Debera Kuntz

PRODUCTION ASSISTANTS Marj Morgan,
Judy Neuenschwander

Library of Congress Control Number:
2012906468
ISBN: 978-1-59635-410-4
1 2 3 4 5 6 7 8 9